A COLLECTOR'S GUIDE TO TEDDY BEARS

A COLLECTOR'S GUIDE TO TEDDY BEARS

PETER FORD

MALLARD
PRESS

MALLARD PRESS
An imprint of BDD Promotional
Book Company, Inc.,
666 Fifth Avenue
New York, New York 10103

Mallard Press and its accompanying design and logo
are trademarks of BDD Promotional Book Company, Inc.
First published in the United States of America in
1990 by the Mallard Press

ISBN 1-792-45349-2

This book was designed and produced by
Quintet Publishing Limited
6 Blundell Street
London N7 9BH

Creative Director: Peter Bridgewater
Art Director: Ian Hunt
Designer: Stuart Walden
Project Editor: Sally Harper
Editor: Elizabeth Nicholson
Photographer: Nick Nicholson

Typeset in Great Britain by
Central Southern Typesetters, Eastbourne
Manufactured in Singapore
by Tien Wah Press (Pte) Ltd

CONTENTS

INTRODUCTION

THE TERM 'ANTIQUE' is sometimes said to mean in its strictest sense an object over 100 years old. By this definition, no teddy bear can be regarded as an antique before the next millennium, as the year 2003 will be the official centenary year of the birth of the teddy bear. On the other hand, antique has in popular usage come to have a far wider application, to the extent where it means almost any item of interest from a period in the past. The antique dealers themselves have meanwhile coined such useful umbrella terms as 'collectables' and 'bygones' to save themselves from getting into any awkward arguments about categories.

Time-spans continually shorten and the habit grows of classifying everything into decades to indicate 'the way we lived then'. Even quite recently outmoded items such as, say, pre-war kitchen implements or fountain pens or early pocket calculators from the 1960s have become collectable. They are sought after by collectors, and as a result command a certain price in the sale rooms in line with their rarity and quality.

Rarity, of course, is a measure of value, and this principle certainly applies in the example of the teddy bear. The German firm of Steiff, for instance, manufactured almost a million toy bears to meet the world demand in 1907, and if all of those teddies survived today, we would still no doubt be able to pick up nice examples in jumble sales at cheap prices. As it is, the great majority of bears, past and present, are loved and battered to bits. It is only the proud survivors which eventually come up for auction at the major sale rooms and fetch a few hundred or even a few thousand pounds or dollars apiece. One illustrious bear that became the world record holder in 1989 sold for £55,000 (nearly $100,000).

There is perhaps no other area of collecting which manages to combine sentiment with expectations of value quite so intensively as that of teddy bears. The idea of collecting teddies is itself captivating, and inevitably it

ABOVE: *A bear showing every sign of a well-loved past.*

RIGHT: *The world's most expensive bear, a 1920 Steiff in dual plush (blond and brown) posing for his pre-auction portrait at Sotheby's (London) when he was only valued at £700-900. He sold for £55,000.*

BELOW: *A set of early bears: the one on all fours is German, c 1907; the little one sitting down is a Yes/No bear, c 1920; and the skittle bear is a rare pre-teddy Steiff bear of 1898.*

FACING PAGE: *Miniature teddys with rabbit companion.*

links in with romantic, mind-haunting memories of teddies previously owned but long lost to spring cleans, hygienic crack-downs and other even more drastic household upheavals and accidents. Meanwhile the idea has taken root that the old family bear, long since retired to the attic, may be worth something more than his nostalgia quotient.

Depending on his circumstances, he may be worth quite a bit or he may be worth very little. Prompted by the publicity that high prices al-

ABOVE: *A splendid hug of bears, owned by Barbara and Beneta Brown of Malvern.*

ways create, bears and their hopeful owners have begun to make regular appearances at 'antiques road show' occasions, and every now and then a valuable and interesting example is brought to light in this way. But alas, expectations turn out more often than not to have been exaggerated.

Without doubt, collectors of teddy bears would stand shoulder to shoulder in supporting the assertion that sentiment is the uppermost motive in their hobby. They talk of the individual personality of certain bears, of how this has been formed not only by the original style of manufacture but also by the way they have

been loved, cuddled, pummelled or used as pillows by their previous owners. Yet whether we like it or not, it is the essentially unsentimental logic of the auction room that defines current values in bears, and that indicates what collectors should expect to pay for examples of specific makes and periods according to condition. Bears are meanwhile in the market place as they have never been before in the whole of their existence.

In every area of present-day collecting, the overall prices at auction continue to pursue an upward trend. This must inevitably have the consequence that certain desirable bears begin to go far beyond the reach and pockets of collectors of modest means. It also means, on the other hand, that there are opportunities for collecting in areas where prices may be expected to rise in future even though they may seem at the moment to be still quite reasonable. In other words, the incipient collector needs to inform himself or herself in every way that is possible about bears and their history. It is most important for them to get to know their teds.

A Collector's Guide to Teddy Bears is designed as a concise introduction, and it assumes no previous knowledge. We should therefore begin with two or three more definitions. Those who collect teddy bears are known as 'arctophiles' (from the Greek, *arkto*, for 'bear', and *philos*, 'friend'), the collecting of bears hence being 'arctophilia'. A group or collection of bears has its collective noun, 'a hug'. And the teddy bear even has its own genus title, *Bruno edwardus*, which may be applied to the true teddy when tracing its line of descent through all the stages of its evolution. In fact, as the range of types of teddy bear grows ever wider, so do the arguments increase among experts as to what the specifications are which make a true teddy. One sometimes has the impression that it is quite rare among arctophiles for anyone actually to get round to asking children what they would say is the best sort of bear from their viewpoint.

In the meantime, those who embark on the collecting of teddy bears have a busy and enjoyable time ahead of them. As they learn their way around bears, they need to look at every sort they can find from every period, and never before have there been so many opportunities for them to do so. There are museums of childhood and there are even whole museums devoted to bears. There are teddy bear events, occasions and picnics promoted by enthusiasts. There are clubs that issue informative newsletters and magazines. There are specialized auction sales and toy fairs. There are other arctophiles to meet up with, talk to and compare notes with up and down the country.

Few people would deny that the spectacle of the most battered example of this distinguished toy, based on a character once called Bruin in honour of his wild origins, but now indelibly known to his friends as Teddy, is certain to rouse a special impulse of warmth in the cockles of the heart.

ABOVE: *A group of three bears, the property of Judy Sparrow.*

LEFT: *An assortment of modern bears with their proud owner indicates the range of teddys now available.*

THE HISTORY OF
THE BEAR

BEARS AND BEAR CULTS

THE HISTORY of the two species, bears and mankind, has intertwined since a very early stage. In nature there are various kinds of bear, ranging from the polar bear of the arctic to the sun bear of Malaysia, to the brown bears of Siberia or Japan, to the grizzly of the Rocky Mountains and the spectacled bear of the Andes. Most bears, the *Encyclopaedia Britannica* informs us, 'enjoy honey'. This fact has at times in certain localities brought bears into conflict with beekeepers, who naturally do not take kindly to having their hives and swarms raided and destroyed.

In the animal kingdom the bear is, of course, a close relative to 'man's best friend' the dog, but bears could never be said to have adapted to domestication in the same way as the dog. A bear cub, like a lion or tiger cub, may well make a captivating pet, but as the creature grows bigger and stronger, so will its wild nature assert itself and the animal become something no longer to be trifled with. Bears have been raised and kept in human communities in various circumstances, but, it also needs to be said, the association could seldom be said to have been to the bears' advantage.

Nevertheless the 'human' characteristics of bears have clearly been important in the way that people have viewed them and used them in myth, legend and entertainment. In his ballad poem 'The Truce of the Bear', Rudyard Kipling tells a powerful tale of the fate of an old bear hunter who once hesitated out of pity to kill his prey. He uses the memorable phrase, 'the Bear that walks like a man'. Bears do walk like men. Their style of walking is plantigrade, the heel of the foot touching the ground first, and at times they walk on their hind legs. 'Even the modern cult of the teddy bear', writes the ethologist James Serpell in his book *In the Company of Animals*, 'testifies to their endearing human-like qualities.' At one time there was actually a

ABOVE: *The primal power of the bear: a polar bear photographed on the ice at Cape Churchill, Manitoba, Canada.*

ABOVE: Another bear at Cape Churchill displays, as he crosses the ice, the hump which nature has given him.

counter-Darwinian theory in circulation which set out to show that the descent of man was from the bear rather than from the ape.

Wherever there has been a close relationship between tribes and a local bear population, so the need to hunt bears for meat and fur invariably seems to have led to rituals to offset the guilt of killing them by granting them the status of divinities. Sixty thousand years ago, Neanderthal man arranged the skulls of bears ritually in caves high in the Swiss and German Alps. The folklore and mythology of the North American Indian tribes are rich in ceremonies and stories relating to bears, these peoples knowing the bear to be 'one of the wisest of animals'. Among the names given to him by the Siberian tribes were 'Grandfather' and 'Worthy Old Man'; the Lapps called him 'King of the Woods' and 'Old Man with Fur Garments'; and to the Ainu of northern Japan he is 'That Divine One Reigning in the Mountains'. The Ainu raised bear cubs as if they were members of the family, treating them as

divine visitors from the spirit world – until the time came for their sacrifice and their return to their spiritual homeland.

It has even been suggested that the shameful spectacle of bear-baiting – setting dogs to attack chained-up bears and to fight to the death in arenas known as bear gardens – was a late survival of the ritual of the sacrificial bear. Bear-baiting in Britain was finally outlawed by an Act of Parliament of 1835, but there were still bears to be seen in the streets and markets, muzzled and chained and trained to dance or turn somersaults.

'Bears is well-behaved enough if they ain't aggravated,' commented an old travelling showman to the great social investigator Henry Mayhew when he was interviewed by him in about 1860. 'Perhaps no one but me is left in England now what properly understands a dancing-bear.' The showman was remembering events from 30 years before, and remarked that his bear, which had been called Jenny, 'wasn't ever baited, but offers was made for it by sport-

ing characters'. Poor Jenny eventually came to grief in Chester, sentenced by the local magistrates to be shot and then sold to the hairdressers, and all because they had continued to play to the crowds one day longer than permitted after a race meeting. 'I couldn't stay to see her shot, and had to go into an alehouse on the road,' said the showman.

In Charles Causley's poem, 'My Mother Saw a Dancing Bear', the children come out of school one hot summer's day to watch a bear being put through its performance, marching, halting and dying for the Queen.

> And then, my mother said, there came
> The keeper with a begging-cup,
> The bear with burning coat of fur,
> Shaming the laughter to a stop.
>
> They paid a penny for the dance,
> But what they saw was not the show;
> Only, in bruin's aching eyes,
> Far-distant forests, and the snow,

ABOVE: *The long muzzle of a grown polar bear shows up clearly in profile.*

LEFT: *At feeding time, the brown bear cubs in the zoo certainly* look *cuddly enough.*

15

It was the sort of sensitivity expressed here, with its response of outrage at the distortion of the bear's true nature, that maybe led to the gradual disappearance of performing bears from the streets. However, bears continued to be accessible, so to speak, for they were exhibited in the travelling menageries, such as Bostock & Wombwell's in England, and found their places in the newly founded zoological gardens of Britain and Europe where they could be kept and studied on the more enlightened grounds of education and science. Thus it may be seen how, from the Dark Ages onward, bears were a part of the experience of ordinary people even in those countries, such as Britain, that had no indigenous bear population.

The anthropomorphic appeal of any animal has invariably led to its gaining a secure place in folk-story and nursery tale. As it was with the selkies, or seal-folk, of the Orkneys, so have male bears been accused, especially in Turkey and Siberia, of kidnapping young women and carrying them away to their secret lairs to be their brides. In Russia the bear has for long been a national symbol, often seized on by cartoonists in times of international tension or conflict. The little bear Mishka is a perennial figure in Russian children's stories, to the extent where he was chosen to be the mascot emblem for the 1980 Olympic Games in Moscow.

In Britain 'The Story of the Three Bears' has been a bedtime favourite ever since Robert Southey, the Poet Laureate of his day, published his version in 1837 in a miscellany of semi-fictional essays entitled *The Doctor &c*. The story was purportedly told by a half-witted old uncle who carried a great store of wonderful stories in his head. For many years it was thought that Southey himself was the originator, making it a rare example of a traditional tale created by an identifiable author. However, in 1894, the folklorist Joseph Jacobs came upon evidence that the story had been in circulation in the oral tradition, and in 1951 a metrical version in a home-made book, predating Southey's by six years, was discovered in a collection of early children's literature in Toronto. In their anthology *The Classic Fairy Tales*, Iona and Peter Opie traced the history of the story. It was a little old woman who originally invaded the bears' house, but in subsequent retellings she evolved through being a little girl called 'Silver Hair' and 'Silver-Locks' until she became 'Goldilocks'.

As the Opies pointed out, 'The Story of the Three Bears' has, as a story type, close affinities with 'Snow White and the Seven Dwarfs', while there is also a Norwegian folk-tale of a princess who discovered a cave inhabited by three bears who happened, in that instance, to change at night into Russian princes. Southey's superb literary treatment of the three bears' story undoubtedly ensured its immortality, and the basic plot has remained constant despite the variations in the nature of its heroine. The bears, too, have remained much the same: a well-ordered family unit with a strong territorial instinct, the precision of whose lives is threatened by chaos through the curiosity and meddling of an intruder. They may seem to be benign, but certainly they are liable to show a dangerous side if crossed.

Apart from the place it holds in legend and story, the bear has also for a long time provided a traditional motif for carvings, ornaments,

FACING PAGE: *Brown bears in a book illustration by C. E. Swan.*

ABOVE: *Kipling's Baloo with Mowgli, from an edition of* The Jungle Book *illustrated by S. Tresilian.*

ABOVE: *A bear smokes a pipe before dancing for his keeper in an illustration from a child's gift book, dating from the 1860s.*

models and children's toys. Among examples which may be mentioned there were the Russian wall-hanging carved toys that raised their legs when a string was pulled. Among the whole range of clockwork automata there were bears that could climb ladders, turn somersaults or simply stalk bear-like across the carpet. There were certainly stuffed toy bears that preceded the coming of the teddy bear, and we know this to be so because a few rare examples have survived. We may therefore well ask how it came about that at one specific point in time a motif which was simply one among many was transformed specifically and phenomenally into what has come to be known and loved as the 'teddy bear'.

It may seem a remote path from the bear cults of our distant ancestors to the bear cult of today's teddy fanciers, but it is possible to trace some intriguing links. The American anthropologist Joseph Campbell has pointed out that the name of King Arthur is derived from the Celtic root for 'bear' and that there was formerly a Celtic god of the same name. More

remarkably the legends of the Germanic hero Dietrich von Berne date from about AD 500, the time of the reign of the Ostrogothic king Theodoric the Great of Verona. It so happens that the place-names Bern and Verona both derive from the German for 'bear' (*Bär*) while Dietrich is the same as Theodoric or Theodore or, in its pet form, 'Teddy'. The name of Theodore, needless to say, turned out to be a most important factor when it came to christening the teddy bear.

· · · · · · · THE BIRTH OF · · · · · · · · · · THE TEDDY BEAR

There are few facts concerning the birth of the teddy bear that have avoided being argued over by experts. Most bear historians are agreed, however, that the year of his birth was 1903 and that his name was given in honour of Theodore Roosevelt who was President of the

ABOVE: *A promenade past the bears' cage at the London Zoo in the 1880s. From* A Panorama of the Zoological Gardens.

LEFT: *The bear pit at Barcelona Zoo in more recent times.*

LEFT: *The story of 'Goldilocks and the Three Bears' provides the theme for a set of Victorian play bricks and their images.*

United States between 1901 and 1909. Apart from that there is almost as much myth and legend involved as there is concerning the bear cults of pre-history. The British counter-claim that it was really King Edward VII, also somewhat on the stout side and known to his friends as Ted, who was the originator of the name, may safely be dismissed as springing from a well-meaning but none too scholarly patriotic impulse. Even so it is open to speculation that the fact that Edward VII was on the throne at the time may have given an extra boost to the new toy's popularity in Britain.

The whole history of invention (whether we are talking about photography, moving pictures, television or penicillin) is rich in examples of rival claims and triumphs based on the work of others. It is often an accident of timing that leads to one person rather than another claiming the credit for any innovation. Teddy bears are no exception in this. Bears in the form of soft toys were certainly being made before 1903. The early part of the story focuses on two family enterprises, a small candy and toy shop in Brooklyn, New York, and a domestic manufactory in the German town of Giengen an der Brenz, some 50 miles (80 km) east of Stuttgart.

In Giengen, a small industrial community dependent on the cloth trade which had developed into being a centre of felt production, there was born in 1847 a girl called Margarete Steiff. She became a polio victim during her childhood. As a result she suffered a paralysis that confined her to a wheel chair, but she was determined never to be an economic burden to her family. She therefore acquired a sewing machine, adapted back to front so she could work the hand wheel with her crippled left hand and guide the cloth with the other, and set herself up as a seamstress.

Her original sense of design expressed itself one day in a flight of fancy. She made a felt pin cushion for her own use in the likeness of an elephant. Those who saw it were enchanted, and before long she found she needed to seek help in making more to keep up with the demand. Before long, it was said, she was producing 5,000 elephants a year. With the range of other stuffed felt animals that she then began to introduce, the family business became such a success that all five of her nephews joined to assist in various capacities. By the time of the Leipzig toy trade fair of 1893 Margarete Steiff was a noted figure in the toymaking world.

FACING PAGE: *An Alaskan brown bear seeks alms in Barcelona.*

ABOVE; *Three miniature bears in a kitchen; a tableau from the Bear Museum at Petersfield, UK.*

FACING PAGE: *A carved Black Forest bear, probably dating from the 1920s, carries a basket on his back.*

The youngest of her nephews, Richard Steiff, had been a student at the local technical college, and had been in the habit of visiting Stuttgart Zoo and the circus to sketch from life likely new additions to the Steiff menagerie. A number of bear models were evidently tried out by the Steiffs, but the considered view was that bears did not set off the same response in the public as certain other animals. Richard, on the other hand, found that bears held a special personal appeal where he was concerned.

Meanwhile, back in Brooklyn, the candy store was being enterprisingly run by its owner, Morris Michtom, an immigrant from Russia (who therefore perhaps had an ancestral feeling for bears). Mrs Michtom was, like Margarete Steiff, a skilled doll and toymaker, and her products were put on sale in the shop as a winning line to help to draw the customers. The day came, on 18 November 1902, when Mr Michtom opened his *Washington Evening Star* to see a cartoon captioned 'Drawing the line in Mississippi'. It showed President Theodore Roosevelt declining to shoot a small captive black-bear cub being restrained on a rope. The cartoon, drawn by Clyfford Berryman, linked

Roosevelt's personal intervention in settling a border dispute between the states of Louisiana and Mississippi with a story about him, perhaps apocryphal, that was then being circulated. On a bear-hunting expedition arranged during the negotiations, the President's hosts in the southern states were said to have been embarrassed by their failure to flush out any bears for him to shoot. All they could find was one pathetic bear cub which they brought tethered into camp. Roosevelt at once declaimed that, 'If I killed this little bear, I could never look my children in the eye again.'

Roosevelt himself had presented a somewhat heroic image to the American people ever since his involvement as leader of the so-called 'Rough Riders' in Cuba during the Spanish-American War of 1898. He had reinforced his robust image with his well-publicized bear-hunting expeditions, for in those days the shooting of big game was still regarded as fit sport for heroes, though today we would mostly take the opposite view. Berryman's cartoon, with its southern political undertones (the black bear) and its implications of the behaviour of a true sportsman, vividly caught the public ima-

RIGHT: *A Vanity Fair cartoon by Flagg of President Theodore Roosevelt.*

gination and gave Mr Michtom an idea. He got Mrs Michtom to make in brown plush fur-like material a bear modelled on the cartoon bear, with movable arms and legs, and this he placed in the shop window alongside the cartoon. In no time, the first Teddy-associated bear had sold and the Michtoms could hardly keep up with the demand that followed.

Shrewdly realizing that he had stumbled on a promising business proposition, Morris Michtom, so legend has it, sent a special presentation bear to the White House with the courtesy request that he give this new type of toy the name of 'Teddy'. The reply came back from the President, so legend continues, 'I don't believe that my name will do much for the image of your stuffed bear, but you have my permission to use it.'

No letters have survived and therefore the facts cannot be verified. As Pam Hebbs, one of the more reliable historians of the teddy bear, has pointed out, the earliest authenticated use of the term 'teddy' only occurs in an American catalogue as late as December 1906. What is indisputable is that this sequence of events culminated by 1907 with the take-off of the

ABOVE: *A restored pre-1910 Steiff bear in excellent shape, held in the London Toy and Model Museum.*

RIGHT: *Three 1930s bears owned by Judy Sparrow.*

FACING PAGE: *Woodcut of a traditional bear, brought back from Moscow by Gyles Brandreth, with a carved bear, probably German, in front.*

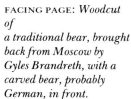

teddy bear craze. This was the year that saw the appearance of the novelty band piece 'The Teddy Bears Picnic', composed by J. E. Bratton, though it was not at that stage provided with the lyrics which are now so familiar. Mr Michtom had meanwhile disposed of his idea to a firm that eventually became the Ideal Toy Company of the present day, but there was no way he could stop the teddy bear entering the public domain and before long there were hosts of imitators.

At about the same time as Roosevelt was arbitrating over state boundaries in the American South, Richard Steiff in Germany was trying to persuade his Aunt Margarete that the firm really ought to reconsider the bear as a toy motif. He had been looking at some of his sketches from several years before and designed a bear with movable head and limbs and fur made of mohair plush. Richard's instinct told him that here would be a toy that a child could really cuddle and respond to. A prototype was even taken to the United States for testing out on American distributors, though it was scornfully received at that stage. With modifications,

the new Steiff bear was made ready to face the world at the Leipzig fair of 1903. It seemed it was destined to be spurned there as well until, on the last day of the fair, a representative of Borgfeldt, New York's leading toy importers, approached the Steiff stand and complained that he had failed to find anything new or interesting in Leipzig that particular year. When Richard Steiff tentatively brought out his new bear – christened 'Friend Petzy', by the way – the man fell on it with joy and placed an order on the spot for 3,000.

By the end of 1903, the Steiff production figures for Petz bears were rising dramatically, and they continued to rise, reaching a peak in 1907 of almost a million. That year is still remembered by the Steiff company, Pam Hebbs tells us, as the 'Year of the Bear' (*Bärenjahre*). One further twist to the tale has yet to be added, however, as the distinguished toy historian, Mary Hillier, has unearthed an apparent English connection with the teddy's genesis after all. In her book *Teddy Bears: a Celebration* she records that a Mr Robinson may also have played a part in encouraging the idea of a plush-

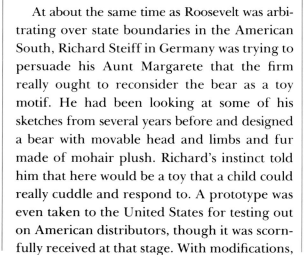

coated bear with Steiff at a time when plush fabric manufactured in Yorkshire was being promoted for use in the making of stuffed toys. Certainly Yorkshire plush played a central role in the character of all the early bears.

Theodore Roosevelt had come to be president through stepping into the breach created by the assassination of President McKinley in 1901. In 1904, when he had to seek election to stay in office, his political aides made much of the bear connection, so bears may well have contributed to the overwhelming victory he gained at the polls. Roosevelt himself evidently came to feel equivocal about teddy bears, on the other hand, and he may in the end have found the whole business a vague embarrassment.

There was one further legend to be woven into the fabric of the myth, and this concerned the wedding of Roosevelt's daughter Alice in 1906. The caterer, it was said, had been at his wit's end to find an appropriate motif for the wedding breakfast decorations until he saw a Steiff bear in a store window and bought up the stock to put on the tables. And this was how, the story continues, all bears in America came to be teddies.

The well-known actor Peter Bull, who became equally well-known as an enthusiastic chronicler of the teddy bear story, was once able to visit Alice Longworth Roosevelt when she was a grand old lady of Washington society. She forbad him to bring any teddy bears to the interview, so Theodore, Peter Bull's constant travelling companion and fortunately a diminutive bear, had to be smuggled in as an eavesdropper in a pocket. Theodore therefore overheard it being said how there had been no bears in sight at the wedding and how this could be demonstrated by the photographs taken of the occasion. Nevertheless it would be impossible to deny that Mr Berryman, who all unwittingly set the whole bear thing going with his cartoon, was fully justified in adopting his own small black bear as a professional trademark for the rest of his working life.

The reason why the notion of the teddy bear took off at the point where it did in history is maybe complex enough to provide material for a university thesis. Perhaps it has, for all we know. The fact that there was a president in the White House called Theodore and a king on the British throne called Edward may have

had at least something to do with it. Perhaps Richard Steiff was correct in thinking that children had reached a point where they needed a toy they could cuddle and that could, at least in their imaginations, cuddle them back. It was the children, after all, who gave the teddy bear their overwhelming vote of confidence and ensured its phenomenal success for what is now not far short of a century. Certainly it seemed as though, in about 1903, the world was simply waiting for the teddy bear to be invented.

FACING PAGE: Bear with miniature violin and earphones.

BELOW: A small Steiff bear (9½ in/24 cm) in white plush, dated to 1905.

②

THE CLASSIC BEAR

WHY BEARS?

AT THE TIME when the world was waiting for the teddy bear, human beings seemed at last to have come up with an idea of the bear which re-created that wild and surly creature of unpredictable reflexes into an image of total benevolence. The fascination with bears that man had felt since the bear cults of prehistory had reached its apotheosis in a child's toy. It must, moreover, have been a toy of special significance, to explain its success and the way it so swiftly established itself in the imaginations of children and their parents.

There is nothing over-simple or too obvious about the teddy bear. One of the original justifications behind its promotion held that it was a sort of 'manly' alternative doll that no little boy need be ashamed of taking to his heart. Playing with dolls would, of course, have been regarded as an unseemly occupation for boys in those days. Surveys have shown, however, that the teddy holds a secure position as the favourite toy for girls between the ages of five and ten.

Psychoanalytic theory would indeed have it that bears represent father figures. A medical director of the Institute of Social Psychiatry in London, Dr Joseph Bierer, has been quoted as saying as much before adding, 'To children they represent goodness, benevolence, kindliness. Parents who replace this cosy, unharmful toy are a menace.' Certainly bears have to take the rough with the smooth and are at times as likely to be punched and kicked as enrolled as confidantes, fellow conspirators or sources of comfort. Hence their need to display that they possess forgiving natures, while the nursery-school bully is quick to realize that one sure way of causing pain to another child is to attack it through its teddy bear.

Love and affection, warmth and softness, assurance – the giving and apparent receiving of these qualities seem to be important elements in the value of the teddy bear as a play-cum-learning toy at a certain stage of personality development. Somehow no other toy manages to do the same job in quite so evocative a way. A teddy may therefore be seen, in one sense, as

ABOVE: *Two Bully bears, one in a sailor hat. Bully bears were created by Peter Bull and produced by the House of Nisbet.*

31

a very superior kind of security blanket, and in that sense the time comes when it is outgrown, discarded and left behind. Yet somehow our teddy bears are never wholly forgotten, and there are adults, who could never be said to be immature or especially eccentric individuals, who retain their bears through all their days and allow them to occupy a special niche in their home and family life.

Nowadays these long-standing relationships are no longer admitted to in the rather secretive or shamefaced way that was once thought appropriate. Such bears have become mascots and needed symbols of security. The teddy fancier no longer needs to fear social disapproval. Too many distinguished people are known to have shared their enthusiasm over the years, while the high prices commanded in the sale rooms make the hobby a perfectly respectable one in the eyes of the world.

LEFT: *A group of teddy bears photographed in the window of a toyshop in York, England.*

RIGHT: *An appealing unmarked Teddy bear in sailor's uniform, made around 1911.*

FACING PAGE: *A well-dressed bear, the property of Barbara and Beneta Brown.*

There have been signs in the past of an anxiety that the residual native fierceness of bears could at some point reassert itself. Steiff continued to provide somewhat redundant leather muzzles to some of their bears before the First World War, but it seems doubtful whether these accessories were ever too popular as bears who still possess their muzzles are now considerable rarities. Even the words to 'The Teddy Bears' Picnic' with which we are familiar – penned by Mr Jimmy Kennedy in 1930 – contain the cautionary notion that if our bears were to get off somewhere together on their own, then feral tendencies might well surface.

In fact it is only occasionally that models of toy bears reach back to create a representation of the bear's true animal nature. Strictly speaking, bears of this sort, however well they are designed and crafted, cannot be regarded as true teddies. The classic figure of *Bruno edwardus* stands out stalwartly and independently. In trying to define the classic bear we shall find ourselves moving steadily further from naturalism for the teddy bear is nothing if he is not a stylized creation.

DEFINING THE CLASSIC BEAR

There are, to begin with, the bears that may be regarded as proto-teddies, though examples of these are few and far between. Among them is a little brown bear, with large ears set low down at the side of his head, that was auctioned at Sotheby's in London in 1984. He was known to date back to before 1903 as his provenance was vouched for by an old lady, by then in her 90s, who had been given him when she was a baby. There were also the so-called 'Peter' bears, manufactured by the firm of Gebrüden Süssenguth at Coburg in Germany. It is often stated for a fact that these particular bears, with their rocking eye and tongue mechanisms and realistically painted teeth, were only manufactured between the years 1925 and 1928, after which they were dropped from production.

This provides an example of how all 'facts' must be treated with caution in questions of teddy bear lore. Pam Hebbs has shown, with the backing of documentary evidence, that a range of these bears was featured in the original

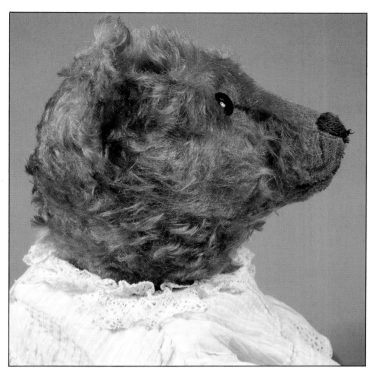

Süssenguth catalogue of 1894. What is beyond all doubt is that they lived up to their maker's claim to be 'most natur-like' *(sic)* with their fur finish, rolling eyes and tongues and displayed teeth, and that as a result they made somewhat alarming nursery companions. A rare and valuable example of a 'Peter' bear was once given to Peter Bull to add to his hug, but it proved to be most unhuggable and not an easy bear to share a home with, and in the end he disposed of it.

What is claimed to be the original Mitchtom 'teddy bear', presented by the Roosevelt family, sits in a glass case in the Smithsonian Institute in Washington, but it is a claim that has come under much critical fire from experts. Whatever the truth in this matter, it is the Steiff bears that set the general standard for the earliest teddy bears, and the resemblance is close between them and all those other bears which are their contemporaries. The Steiff bears were highly distinctive but also immensely influential. It may even be true that certain small bears in particular have in the past been auctioned as Steiffs when they were the products of other firms whose names are by this stage unidentifiable or even forgotten. The great majority of early bears were made either in Germany or the United States, and the Steiff bears were among the top sellers. The way a Steiff bear looks is therefore the first thing with which any collector ought to become familiar. It needs to be empha-

sized that it is impossible to make too close a study of bears and their different characteristics as these have been introduced by their makers at various periods.

The profile of the early Steiff bear runs as follows. He gazes at us with black boot-button eyes along a sharpish muzzle, trimmed of its plush, that ends in a well-stitched wool nose above an inverted 'V' for a mouth. He has a distinctly humped back to testify to his origins in the wild. His arms are long, and as he stands there, between perhaps 18 and 30 inches (45 and 75 cm) high, they hang down almost to where his knees would be if he had any. His front paws and feet are large, his legs taper towards his feet from broadly placed thighs, his feet are set at right angles to his legs, and his claws or toes may well be represented by black wool stitches. All his limbs are jointed and movable, attached sideways on at the shoulders and hips. He can sit with his legs stretched out or he can raise his paws above his head if he wishes, or else he can stretch out his arms in an appealing gesture. In so doing he will display the felt or velvet pads on his paws and feet.

His head pivots in a similar way to his limbs and he has the great advantage of being able to turn it through 360 degrees so he can look backwards behind him. The rather loose type of jointing that was originally used for his movable parts was, incidentally, quite soon to

FACING PAGE: *A pair of early Steiff bears to whom time has given a touching individuality.*

ABOVE LEFT AND RIGHT:
The profiles of the smaller and the larger bear respectively.

be replaced by an improved system using discs or stiff cardboard. His fur is, as a rule, made of mohair plush (a fabric distinguished from velvet by its longer and looser pile) in a range of natural shades from beige to brown, and his rather un-yielding body is stuffed with wood shavings or sawdust. Excelsior was the proprietary name for a patented type of fine, curly wood shavings much used in early stuffed toys. Sometimes his stomach is fitted out with a 'growler' that, if it is still in working order, emits a noise when he is turned on his head, though the noise itself has in some quarters been considered a bit of a joke since it sounds more like a cow mooing than anything else.

ABOVE LEFT: *A Steiff button survives* in situ *in its owner's left ear.*

BELOW LEFT: *A pair of Steiff bears in blond plush dating from 1908.*

There is one other detail which needs to be mentioned. He has a metal button in his left ear. This is the famous *Knöpf im Ohr* ('button in ear'), a registered trade mark device settled on by Margarete Steiff in 1904 to reassure customers that such bears were genuine products of her workshops. The button originally held a label in place, and it might be blank or it might have the name 'STEIFF' die-stamped on it in capital letters. It is very likely to be made from a pewter alloy. Most labels and many buttons were probably detached by parents, for safety's sake, before the bears were handed over to children, but examples do occasionally emerge with labels as well as buttons intact. It is more common for the button alone to still be in position, but in the course of events many genuine Steiff bears are today buttonless. It has also been known for straying Steiff buttons to become attached to the ears of non-Steiff bears in the hope of raising values. The Steiff button does therefore have its problematic aspects for the collector.

The above portrait of a bear is a generaliza-

tion, and it has to be remembered that variations on the basic specifications start to appear from the very beginning. It nevertheless represents the fundamental pattern, back to which all later developments need to be related.

We have so far referred to the bear as 'he' in line with the father-figure theory, and most owners of bears will tend to think of their unclothed charges as 'Mr' rather than 'Mrs'. It would be a bad day for bears though, if the contentious issues of sexism were to surface in the world of arctophilia. Teddy bears are on the whole remarkably androgenous figures, as dressing them in different styles of clothes will demonstrate. They are only too willing to be whatever gender their owners would like them to be and can on the whole look as convincing in a frock as in trousers. Manufacturers have, in more recent years, tried to come up with 'gentleman bear' and 'lady bear' casts of face

for ready-dressed models or families of bears.

Labels, trade marks and tokens may clearly be of the utmost importance in dating examples of bears, as may changes and developments in their physical characteristics. These questions will be gone into in more specific detail in Chapter Eight. Meanwhile we are mainly concerned with the broad outline of bears, and the phases it has passed through to produce the bear that would be recognized as typical by the greatest number of people today. The focus here, for various reasons, must be on the way the bear evolved between the First and the Second World Wars. Social circumstances have had their influence on bears, especially in times of war, when traditional trading patterns have been interrupted and manufactured materials have been in short supply, but the bear was changing slowly and surely in any case.

If the bear craze had its beginning in the

ABOVE: *Clockwork Byng bear on a swing, c 1910.*

RIGHT: *A group of pre-1930 Schuco bears of assorted colours.*

United States in 1902 and spread to Britain a while later (the term 'teddy' emerges in no trade catalogues in Britain before 1909) it was not really damped down until the outbreak of the First World War. By that time bears had literally begun to take on a new look. Boot-button eyes, stitched into place, had given way to glass eyes with pupils, anchored into the head by long spikes or wires. Various later dates than this have sometimes been authoritatively put forward for the introduction of glass eyes, but a Sears Roebuck catalogue for 1912 states that its finest quality German plush bears were at that time 'all fitted with glass eyes'.

The range of shades used to make a bear's fur had widened and in some cases become quite unusual, but the main changes did not really get going until the return of peace in the 1920s. Teddy bears then took their place in the flapper age and colourful wardrobes became quite the fashion. Providing bears with complete outfits of clothes was nothing new in itself however. That had begun to happen in the earliest days of the teddy bear craze in 1906. The overall profile also started to change after the war, the hump at last beginning to modify (though not yet to disappear entirely). The limbs began to shorten, the feet to become less prominent (by the end of the 1930s), and the torso to grow stouter in outline. Rexine began to replace felt or velvet on paw pads, while noses at times grew black and hard when they happened to be made from gutta-percha. When the hump finally went out of vogue, some elderly bears found themselves being let in for plastic surgery.

As rounded curves became far more popular for bears, the bear profile softened, as did the types of stuffing used to pad him out. Kapok by this time began to be used far more widely. The result was all the while moving towards a more cuddly bear and one that might suffer no hurt if he should, for instance, fall off the ottoman or get dragged bumping down the stairs. Intimately involved in all such developments was one particular highly influential bear:

Our Teddy Bear is short and fat,
Which is not to be wondered at.
A bear, however hard he tries,
Grows tubby without exercise.

He still had a bit of a hump, as the drawings of him by E. H. Shepard showed, and his name

ABOVE: *A group of Judith Sparrow 'Big Theodore' resin bears.*

of course was Edward Bear, alias Winnie the Pooh. A A. Milne's four classic children's books were published in the 1920s in this order: *When We Were Very Young* (1924), *Winnie the Pooh* (1926), *Now We Are Six* (1927) and *The House at Pooh Corner* (1928).

The eponymous hero of the two sets of Pooh

sets of Pooh stories therefore became for several generations a special and particular image of what a bear should be, though Shepard made him such a strong individual that he could never have been mistaken for any other bear. Winnie the Pooh is thus both unique and representative.

The original model for the stories was

ABOVE LEFT: *Close-up of Brother Ted, a jester bear of 1927.*

BELOW LEFT: *Brother Ted shows off his motley colour scheme in a full-length portrait.*

Christopher Robin Milne's own bear, which was close in appearance to the Steiff standard for bears. When he came to draw the character, however, E. H. Shepard used 'Growler', his own son's bear – a 1906 Steiff bear, it so happens – as his starting point, and developed Pooh creatively from there. The well-rounded bear that emerged from the Pooh revolution was to provide the foundation for the next generation of bears in the years following the Second World War.

Any one impression of a 'classic' bear is always essentially transitional, but if the 1920s and 1930s were the hey-day of the classic bear, then the shadow of the basic Steiff is still there behind it, to help us maintain a definitive notion.

When that indefatigable arctophile Peter Bull was invited by a toy firm, the house of Nisbet, to come up with the specifications for his idea of the perfect teddy, free from all gimmicky accretions, he went for a long muzzle and a hump and 'that woollen embroidery for the pads and the paws'. The fact that children liked 'to

pick at the embroidery and then it's hell for the poor parent to knit on again' was, in his view, all part of the fun. The result was Bully Bear, a classic teddy if ever there was one, launched commercially by a party at the British House of Commons in October 1980. Time and time again, whenever we try to pin down the classic features, we find them in the original bear that Richard Steiff designed for his Aunt Margarete.

BELOW: *A Steiff wheeled bear, meant to be ridden on, c 1918. He is steerable and provided with a ring-pull growler.*

TALL, SHORT AND MOBILE

The classic bear in his ascendancy had three other manifestations: the large bear, the miniature bear and the bear on wheels. The large bear could be large indeed, as large as, or larger than, his owner. He could be a piece of conspicuous vulgarity standing maybe four or five feet (one and a half metres) tall. Some were manu-

factured to be centre pieces for trade displays in the toy departments of big stores before Christmas and sold to ostentatious nurseries.

The miniature bear, by contrast, had a far more cultivated pedigree. Steiff was producing bears as small as nine inches (22 cm) high by 1905, but the true miniatures are six inches (15 cm) or less. In the 1920s the Nuremberg firm of Schreyer was producing a notably characteristic type of bear that was only 2⅜ inches (6

cm) high, built on a rigid patent metal frame but covered in soft mohair.

The bears on iron wheels were made large enough for a child to ride on their backs, and were altogether closer to the wild bear, being down on all fours. Sometimes they were covered in blanket material, but the better-quality ones had coats of mohair plush. Steiff had always produced a range of wheeled animals, so naturally there were bears among them.

ABOVE: *Paddington Bear and his Aunt Lucy make the acquaintance of a newly dressed and sinisterly smiling Sussengüth 'Peter' bear.*

3

THE AUTOMATED BEAR

ABOVE: *German automaton dancing bears on a wind-handle musical box as well as a wind-up tinplate walking bear.*

THE MOVING BEAR

THE HISTORY of the automated bear is more closely tied in, at the outset, with the development of the automaton toy than with the history of *Bruno edwardus*. There were reputedly automata in Ancient Greece, while in eighteenth-century Europe clockmakers built ingeniously devised and much-admired mechanical men. Automation in toys is something that has always followed close on the heels of wider developments in science. It can perhaps be seen as a relatively frivolous application of serious new technological principles or inventions. Clockwork toys of enamelled tin, cheaply mass-produced and as often as not made in Germany, became common nursery ornaments during the later Victorian era. Among the manic clowns, the performing dogs and cats, the trick cyclists, jugglers and acrobats, there were also bears which went through their acts and stunts. Any one of these today will be highly prized as a collectors' piece.

It becomes clear that collectors of bear material cannot always expect to have an exclusive interest in the field. At certain points they are going to find themselves in direct rivalry with collectors in other areas. A performing or dancing bear is going to represent as choice an item for the collector of tin automata as it will for the bear enthusiast. All such vintage items are attractive and charming and cannot fail to bring out acquistive instincts in the eyes of those who spot them in sale rooms and specialist shops. Therefore prices are high today, especially for well-preserved pieces in working order.

The bear was, in this context, only one animal in a whole menagerie of examples. If we are now singling out the bears it is because of the attention they have drawn to themselves through the extraordinary teddy bear phenomenon. The same comment may be said to apply to those wall-hanging, wood-crafted toys with movable limbs that jerk up and down when you pull a string attached to their backs. Sometimes the motif used for these was a bear, especially in Russia, and toys in the form of a bear have added collectability.

There was also, however, another type of mechanical toy that was specifically a bear, individually built and given a covering of authentic fur to hide his mechanism. Originally these sometimes startlingly realistic creations performed technical displays that were intended

RIGHT: *Two wooden carved Russian bears. The one with the wooden ball moves its arms and washes its young in a tub; the other works by a push/pull device to bang in a nail.*

FACING PAGE: *Russian clockwork clapping bear, with original box.*

much more for the drawing room than for the nursery. Mass-produced versions soon followed, including among them bears that would walk on all fours or on their hind legs, bears that would dance, bears that would climb ladders, tumble on the floor or perform somersaults on a trapeze.

Outstanding examples of such bears were produced by the German firm of Gebrüder Bing of Nuremberg, kitchenware manufacturers who branched out into tin clockwork toys at about the turn of the century. Bing bears, fully mechanical or simply with jointed limbs, were quite close to the Steiff convention in appearance, though with smaller ears and slightly flatter noses. They also had a metal tag clipped on to their ears – rather like the identification tags farmers use on cattle today. At first the tags had the initials 'G.B.N.', which stood for Gebrüder Bing Nürnberg, though soon after the First World War this was changed to 'B.W.' for Bing Werke. Bing bears were renowned

for being splendidly and colourfully dressed, but they are rare and valuable enough as they stand and examples with their original clothes intact are few and far between indeed.

The Bing company went into liquidation early in the 1930s, but mechanical bears continued to be manufactured by the toy industry, latterly by the Japanese, in great quantities until the reign of the clockwork toy began its final decline in the 1960s. Along with so much else in the lives of succeeding generations, the key-wound clockwork mechanism became an outmoded piece of technology, ready to be replaced by friction gears and battery-powered electronics.

THE TALKING BEAR

The Sussengüth bears, already described in the previous chapter, possessed a simple automated feature in their moving eyes and tongues. The most rudimentary piece of automation of all, however, was the 'growler', the device in the

МЕХАНИЧЕСКАЯ ИГРУШКА
ТАНЦУЮЩИ
МЕДВЕДЬ
Артикул ЛГ-085-01-51
СДЕЛАНО В СССР

ABOVE: *A pipe-smoker and a drummer: two Japanese battery-operated tin automaton bears.*

stomach to enable a bear to make a theoretically growly noise when he was rocked from side to side or turned topsy-turvy. Sometimes squeakers were used instead, which put out a noise whenever the stomach was pressed in. A venerable bear, needless to say, will not always have a growler or squeaker in operative order.

Growlers went through various stages of improvement after the early rather unsatisfactory Steiff ones, and in the 1920s the English firm of Chad Valley was producing ranges of bears which were fitted with what was called the 'Chad Valley patent growler'. Squeakers and growlers come to seem exceedingly primitive devices in comparison with later developments. The most recent chapter in the history of the growler in fact is the techno-bear of the present day, whose insides conceal a micro-chip cassette player that equips him with a vocabulary of up to 400 words in variable order.

Such gimmicks would doubtless have been deplored by the late Peter Bull, for whom the whole business of communication with bears took place on an altogether more elevated plane of the imagination. As a general principle, of course, classic toys of all types have a wonderful simplicity that represents a challenge to a child's imaginings and is most important in the development of those capacities. The marvels of science let loose in the land of toys can all too often be an impoverishment rather than an enrichment: an adult notion of what a child ought to like rather than what a child actually needs. In this respect, Peter Bull's instincts would most certainly be correct. The irony is that, in a deep sense, a chatterbox bear may be far less effective as a communicator than a bear which sits and looks back at you with boot-button eyes. The bear, as a highly developed marketable novelty product, actually seems to be in the process of losing his human appeal. In the end that appeal surely all depends on the qualities of the classic bear, however much that bear may have lost bits of his stuffing.

ABOVE LEFT: *A fierce-looking open-mouthed clockwork walking bear with a coat of real fur.*

BELOW LEFT: *A tricycle bear and a scooter bear, both dating from the 1930s.*

In their book *Teddy Bears*, the French bear historians, Geneviève and Gérard Picot, give an account illustrating the appeal of the techno-bear in certain adult circles. They describe an occasion when prototype bears of two different sorts were handed-out to delegates at a conference in the United States.

Those given to the men were dressed in a pin-striped suit, white shirt and red tie and, when activated, said in a deep voice: 'You are on the path to success, you're a born winner.' Women were given bears dressed in a white suit with a striped red blouse, and which gently murmured: 'Be what you want to be. You're perfect, absolutely perfect. Mr Bear says you're a winner.'

It seems a sad day when we hear of teddy bears being dragooned into telling the yuppie generation not the truth about itself but only what it wishes to hear. It is even sadder to learn that these craven bears achieved over half a million in sales.

NOVELTY AND LISTENING BEARS

The novelty bear began to put in an appearance early on in the days of the bear craze. In the years leading up to the First World War, Pam Hebbs tells us, bears became capable of all manner of activities: 'they growled, they cried, they nodded their heads, they ran on wheels. There were teddy bears whose eyes lit up electrically.' Peter Bull in his book *Book of Teddy Bears* quotes a firm called the Fast Black Skirt Company as advertising in this period 'Electric

BELOW: *A pair of Schuco wind-up ice-cream eating bears with plush coats and glass eyes.*

FACING PAGE: *The 'Great Roaring Bear', a Japanese clockwork toy with synthetic fur and its original box.*

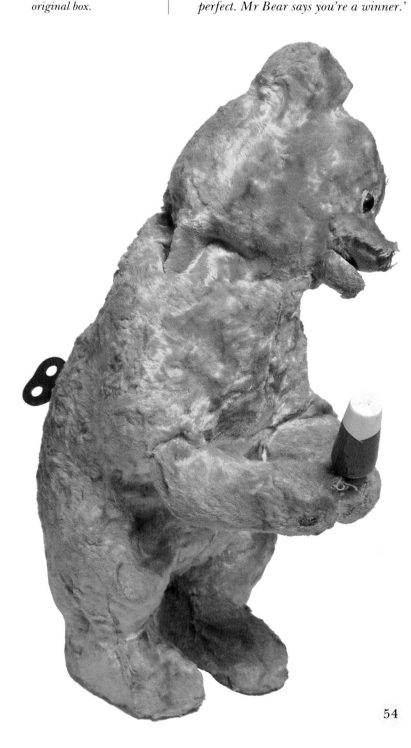

JAPAN

GIANT ROARING BEAR

LEFT: *Two mechanical bears: one can knit, the other can read.*

Bright-Eye Teddy Bears – Shake the Right Paw, Eyes Light Up White or Red'.

The onset of the war called a temporary halt to the flow of innovation, but it was on the move again soon after peace was declared. The 'electric eye bear' itself clearly continued to represent a thoughtless hazard for small children – a case of ingenuity outstripping basic safety requirements. The Sears Roebuck catalogue for 1919 included an emphatic statement on why the company would neither stock nor sell such bears: '. . . up to the present, we have not found one that will give entire satisfaction. The batteries soon wear out and the small bulb glass eyes break easily. We recommend plain bears.'

It was also at about the close of the war that the firm Schreyer und Co. built a new factory in Nuremberg to specialize in the manufacture of mechanical toys as well as of the famous miniature bears already described in Chapter Two. Through the company's trademark,

'Schuco', their range of bears came to be known as Schuco bears, the so-called 'Yes/No' bear being a product that was specific to the company. By twisting the tails of these bears, you could make their heads nod for an affirmative or shake for a denial. Certainly this engagingly simple device opened up possibilities of games that might be played with bears, such as asking whether one's porridge was still too hot to eat, and they continued to appear in various manifestations. One of the most appropriate of the 'Yes/No' bears was the bell-hop bear, who was dressed in a smart red jacket and the round red cap of a hotel page. An alternative version was a bear whose tail merely made the head swivel so he seemed to be looking about the room (a 'No/No' bear).

Apart from these there were, among others, the usual walking or somersaulting bears and a skating bear who would have looked very fine as he used the linoleum as a skating rink. The trade-name 'Schuco' appeared on the keys used

FACING PAGE: *Three Schuco bears from the 1930s: the one sitting is a Yes/No bear, the one standing is a dancing bear, and the lilac bear is a Schuco miniature, 3½ in (8.7 cm) high.*

RIGHT: *A musical-box bear with a train that goes round and round to the accompaniment of a Disneyland tune.*

FACING PAGE: *Drinking companions: the smaller bear is clockwork and the larger one is battery driven.*

BELOW: *The 'Minic' walking bear, with original box, manufactured by Triang.*

to wind the clockwork, but in the nature of things the majority of these have been lost. Schuco bears are, even so, highly recognizable for their jaunty panache and excellent quality.

Schreyer's went into eclipse in 1936 because the toys, together with their originators, fell victim to the Nazi persecution of the Jews. The firm of Schreyer was revived in the postwar years and achieved considerable sales in North America through one of the directors, who had managed to escape from the terror in Europe, and had set up a subsidiary import company in the United States. Schuco bears from all periods are today highly collectable items.

When Schreyer's eventually went into liquidation in the early 1970s, it was because they could no longer compete with the boom in toy-

making that originated in the Far East, from Japan and Taiwan in particular. Since the 1950s, Japanese toymakers had been vigorously exporting to the world all sorts of clockwork bear automata, including such devices as shoe-shine bears and bears that sit writing at desks. Good examples of these, too, have now come to be firmly ensconced under the heading 'collectable'.

It needs to be said that Steiff have also made mechanical and tumbling bears at various times, as well as bears with voice boxes and musical bears that may be regarded as an extension of the voice-box principle. Some bears may essentially be music boxes dressed up to look like teddies. In examples of earlier tin-plate toys, the bear may be simply a revolving ornament on top of a musical box. Other bears are little

LEFT: *A fine mechanical clown bear with juggling ball and stick effect, manufactured by Moses Kohnstamm, Furth, Germany, in the 1920s.*

FACING PAGE: *An English Leco bear is metamorphosed as a musical box; it also has a head movement.*

more than a particularly fancy kind of alarm clock. Yet other bears have hearts that beat inside their chests, while the introduction of the cassette player into doll making has meant, as we have seen, that bears today can talk to us, ask for honey or tell us stories. They may also sing lullabies to put us to sleep or even launch into renderings of the 'Teddy Bears' Picnic'.

What Peter Bull called his 'most unfavourite refinement' in this area was a bear with a transistor tape concealed in its head. The owner could press one button and speak to the bear, then press another button, upon which the eyes would light up and the bear speak the very same words back in a voice transformed into a gravelly growl. Of such mutations Mr Bull had this to say:

Their very modernity turns them into some slightly spookey animal who is neither one thing nor the other and of whom one can never be sure. One can't imagine them listening or just Being Quiet. Friendship seems to be out of the question because in some way they attract too much attention to themselves.

Peter Bull feared that the manufacturers would never cease trying to demonstrate how they were managing to keep up with the times, and each new season in the toy trade will doubtless see many fresh wonders unveiled. True arctophiles, one suspects, will always tend to remain sceptical of whether the specifically new can ever add anything of much significance to the basic legend.

4

THE ADAPTED BEAR

INFLUENCES ON THE BEAR

T HE TEDDY BEAR, having become an indispensable accessory to childhood in the eyes of so many adults, has gone through a far vaster number of adaptations and permutations than any brief text could hope to cover. Parents feel that a teddyless childhood must also be a deprived childhood and so, in times of war, we have had teddies of all kinds, utilizing oddments of material or wool, cut out or knitted following bought patterns, or simply improvised out of the inspiration of their individual makers. It becomes a perfectly natural thing to think that the teddy may help to soothe anxieties in stressful circumstances, and the image of the evacuee or refugee child clutching its teddy bear on a journey into the unknown takes on a special poignancy.

To make your own bear, of course, is to ensure that you really can have a bear that is unique. Even if you are using a bought craft pattern, and there are always some available, you can slip in your own variations, colour schemes and so on. Charming, quaint and touching examples of bears handmade by amateurs – knitted bears, crocheted bears, rag bears, felt or cloth bears – can and do turn up in jumble sales, charity shops and craft fairs.

In France, during the time of the Vichy government and the German occupation, there was a curious anomaly in that import quotas did not cover sheep hides from North Africa. A consequence of this was the appearance of a type of French bear of sheepskin (similar bears were also made in Britain).

Other factors besides social expediency have had a profound influence over how bears are

ABOVE: *A teddy takes off into rainbow colours, co-ordinated with his owner's style of dress.*

TEDDY BEAR, PRAM BALL & RED RIDING HOOD DOLL'S SET
(Oddments of 3 and 4-ply)

BESTWAY LEAFLET 604 3ᵈ

RIGHT: *A Bestway pattern book from the 1940s includes a pattern for a knitted bear as well as for a pram ball and a 'Red Riding Hood' outfit for a doll.*

FACING PAGE: *A knitted bear, probably French, dating from c 1960.*

made, at times to the point of altering their nature quite fundamentally. Eyes, in recent years, have tended to be plastic rather than glass. Noses, too, have become plastic in most bears mass-produced for the wider market. Technological advance and the development of man-made fibres have meant that there are now bears that may be put through a wash in a washing machine without sustaining any harm either to their fur or their stuffing. Synthetic fibres have also led to synthetic colours, most hectically perhaps in the Care Bear series, whose neon shades of fur, overstated cuteness and names like 'Good Luck Bear' and 'Funshine Bear' have made most arctophiles explode in indignation. One wonders what children, who

are the people who ought to be asked, actually make of them.

Health and safety regulations have similarly had a far-reaching influence on the way bears are manufactured and they now govern what materials a bear should be stuffed with and made from. The idea of the benign teddy being a threat to health and well-being naturally goes against the grain, but many period teddies would no doubt fail the test of up-to-date specifications. Their fur and fabric need to be flame-proof. They should not begin to give off toxic fumes if placed too close to a fire. Makers should avoid eyes that may be easily pulled out leaving spikes or sharp wires exposed. Bears should be robust at the seams to resist being

RIGHT: *The softening profile of an English bear of the 1930s.*

FACING PAGE: *A group of modern bears mix traditional design with a more cuddly appearance.*

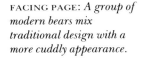

torn apart, especially if their innards contain sharp-edged mechanisms or equipment that the curious-minded infant may try to extract. Dyes and colourings should, needless to say, hold fast against sucking and be non-toxic.

It sometimes happens that imported toys, including bears with lethal eye spikes or made of highly flammable materials, do find their way on to the market, especially close to Christmas time. This gives us one good reason for never buying temptingly cheap bears from street traders. They may turn out to be treacherous companions. As soon as they are discovered, they usually have to be swiftly withdrawn.

The various types of latex stuffing used since the 1950s have perhaps had the greatest influ-ence of all over the most recent revolution in the bear's profile, and have led to an ever-increasing cuddliness. The trend towards softer, rounder, dumpier but more lightweight bears has continued. Jointed arms, legs and necks have often disappeared, leading naturally to positively floppy bears that tumble about or are able to drape themselves over the backs of upholstered chairs. The tactile quality of more recent bears — their warmth and responsive suppleness and softness — brings us closer to the notion of what may be regarded as the psycho-logically correct teddy. We are speaking here of the bear to which a child may best respond and which may give back most in the process. We are even speaking of the therapeutic bear.

THE BEAR AS THERAPIST

The teddy that reproduces a heartbeat in his breast is a case in point, as the originator of a reassuring primal rhythm that relates to life. On an even more primal topic, tests have been carried out in the United States in which infants between the ages of one week and four months old were given special bears. The bears, known as Dakin 'Rock-a-Bye Baby' bears, were equipped to reproduce the sounds heard by a foetus securely floating in the amniotic fluid. It was shown that these bears can have a soothing affect on babies who are going through their initial sixteen-week period of adjustment to being out in the great wide world.

In this context, we need to consider carefully if briefly what the function of a teddy bear may be in a child's life. All experts concerned with the subject of childcare acknowledge the importance of toys in the child's emotional as well as its learning development. A favourite toy (which, as we have seen, is extremely likely to be a teddy) is a so-termed 'transitional object'. This means that it can be expected to assist a young child through difficulties, such as the fear of separation from its mother. It can provide reassurance against deprivation, or the anxieties of being alone at bedtime or being in a strange place in unusual circumstances. It can also act as a catalyst in testing out, through play, the real business of social exchange and response, the giving of affection and the assertion of the personality. In other words, the toy can help the child to cope with life.

The bear as sharer of experience is central to the whole idea of the bear as therapist. One of Peter Bull's many correspondents told him of a bear that had been made with the rudimentary arms of a thalidomide victim. He blenched personally at this, thinking it was going altogether too far with the principle of identification, but it would nevertheless be interesting to know how successful that particular bear was in carrying out the task for which it was designed. Bears have for many years been prominent among the occupants of children's wards in hospitals, where they have undertaken sterling service. They have submitted to being bandaged up and given unpalatable medicines and put through practically anything a child in hospital may have to endure, including surgery

with its aftermath of scars and stitching. There are many vouched-for anecdotes to show how the constant presence of a bear at a bedside has encouraged a child through a dangerous illness. The famous bear manufacturing company of Merrythought were at one time even commissioned to build a teddy that could, through a system of tubes, administer an anaesthetic and so deflect attention from the alarming paraphernalia in the operating theatres of those days.

LEFT: *A teddy bear gives support to a small boy during the serious business of a hospital consultation.*

It would be hard to imagine a more utterly benevolent piece of philanthropy than the work which seeks to fulfil the vision of the late Mr Russell McLean, known to posterity as 'The Teddy Bear Man'. Mr McLean lived in the city of Ohio and knew more than most about what it was like to be a child in hospital as he had himself suffered from health problems since an early age. He therefore conceived the idea of presenting a teddy to every child who was admitted to the children's wards in the two city hospitals. Initially he was able to tap a state sales-tax arrangement that made money available to charity, until his scheme took off – in part with the support of a local television company – and it became entirely self-financing from an unfailing flow of donations.

Only a few years before he died in 1969, Russell McLean was able to present his 50,000th bear to a child. The letters of thanks he received

ABOVE: *A teddy gas-mask case to take the type of gas mask issued to young children in Britain during the early stages of the Second World War.*

FACING PAGE: *A pair of colourful resin bears.*

during his lifetime were many, but the following example is typical:

I didn't think much of your project at first. I thought all those children already have a favourite toy. What could a new little Teddy do? Then I found out. Our four-year-old child had an accident and was completely terrified at finding herself hospitalized. Then came that little Teddy at a time when nothing else would have done. Our girl is grown-up now but she still has that Teddy.

The example of Mr McLean's work has since been built on and extended by a broadcaster and journalist, Mr Jim Ownby, who in 1973 founded, from where he worked in Hawaii, the organization known as the Good Bears of the World. Its objective was (and still is) to provide the comfort of bears to all children in distressed circumstances in hospitals and institutions wherever they may happen to be. The British branch has made bears available in many hospitals, whose staff will confirm the unique therapeutic value of these beneficent creatures. In such an enterprise the dedicated arctophile will recognize a cause dear to the heart.

BEAR'S FRIENDS AND CLOSE RELATIONS

Stories written about bears as well as film (especially cartoon) creations and children's series on television have all had a far-reaching influ-

ence on the range of bear types available in toy shops during the postwar years. Whether these characters always qualify as teddy bears in the strictest sense of the term is a matter for debate, but they are clearly entitled to a place in any account of the modern bear cult.

Literary bears in all their manifestations are discussed in the next chapter. Bears that originate with a television series are designed primarily as a merchandisable product that takes advantage of a programme's following. An example of a bear that became an enormous

commercial success after appearing on television was the late Harry Corbett's little yellow glove-puppet known as Sooty. Mr Corbett first caught sight of him in a shop on the North Pier at Blackpool. He was at the time doing a magic act for children's parties in his spare time in the evenings, and was at once struck with the idea that the little puppet would make a good assistant. 'I just couldn't leave him', Mr Corbett was reported as saying, 'he looked so appealing.' The original Sooty cost him 7s. 6d. (35p or about 60 cents in today's money).

A few years later a chance appearance on television led to contracts and stardom. Mr Corbett promptly left behind his more prosaic career as an engineer surveyor, blacked up the little puppet's ears so he would show up to better advantage on the television screen (still no colour in those days) and proceeded to entrance more than a generation of children. Many of those who watched and revelled in the antics of this naughty little bear who, aided and abetted by Sweep, the floppy-eared dog, created chaos in the midst of all Mr Corbett's attempts to show the public some magic tricks, also had the chance to possess their own versions of Sooty and his friend Sweep, not to mention Soo, the little girl panda who also featured in the programme. They still do, for Mr Corbett's son Matthew has continued with his father's work.

In France, it was the character of Gros Nounours who had a comparable television career, that, from his introduction in the 1960s, lasted for over a thousand episodes. Gros Nounours is thought to have derived from the earlier character of Teddy in the English 'Andy Pandy' series. As a contrast with Sooty's unruly clowning, however, Gros Nounours was in collusion with the Sandman to persuade all good little children to go peaceably to bed once he had told them a story. It is said that he single-handedly tripled the figures for the sales of teddy bears in France for the year 1962 alone. His series eventually came to an end, but his myth lives on.

Where cinema is concerned, the influence of Walt Disney has of course been considerable, especially in his celluloid re-creations of two famous bears: A. A. Milne's Winnie the Pooh and Baloo, the bear from Rudyard Kipling's *The Jungle Book*. Whether or not one cares greatly for these re-creations (in Britain they have certainly tended to be disowned as traves-

BELOW: A Sooty on a tricycle and a glove-puppet Sooty, both manufactured by Chad Valley.

ABOVE: Mike Harding's Superted, ever ready to undertake a good deed.

ties of their original spirit), Disney Poohs and Baloos have appeared on the shelves of toy shops and department stores all over the world, and therefore cannot be entirely cold-shouldered. The day will after all come when they, too, are vintage bears.

A recent character who owes his popularity to his appearance as much on film as in books is Mike Young's Superted. Like his heroic human precursor, he flies to the gallant rescue in a series of adventures. His fictional history is as a former reject from a toy factory who was stumbled over by the spaceman Spottyman and sprinkled with a magic dust. Rather like the Sooty glove puppets, and the Disney Poohs and Yogi Bears based on the Hanna Barbera cartoons, Superted models are made for the fans. This may set them slightly apart in the teddy bear phenomenon since they are owned

FACING PAGE: *Two rare French mechanical bears: the dancing one on the right dates from c 1890 and the ladder-climbing one was manufactured c 1910.*

ABOVE: *Because of its rarity and unique appeal, the giant panda of China became an archetypal symbol of conservation.*

OVERLEAF, LEFT: *A young polar bear evokes the appeal of his kind.*

OVERLEAF, RIGHT: *A swivel-headed polar bear of the 1950s, inspired by the birth of Brumas, the first polar-bear cub to be born in captivity, in the London Zoo in 1949.*

for what they represent rather than for their own sakes. Even so, Superted is of interest in that he introduces a positive element into the protective powers of bears. In terms of the central teddy bear tradition, Superted may be considered to take these powers to too great an extreme, but he carries his moral heart in the right place.

What, therefore, of those other animals that are more or less bear-like but not quite bears? The teddy polar bear is by no means uncommon as a variant and may be seen as firmly belonging with the tribe of *Bruno edwardii*, but then there are also pandas, who are cousins to bears in the evolutionary scale of things. The panda as a stuffed toy only began to make an appearance from 1936 onwards, since that was the year when Su-Lin, the first of China's rare giant pandas to come and live in a Western zoo, arrived in the United States. The panda motif has been given a further boost in more recent times through being adopted as the symbol of the World Wildlife Fund (recently renamed the World Wide Fund for Nature), and hence it has become a symbol of conservation in general.

Badgers, too, are cousins to bears, though the badger as a stuffed toy seems, with its characteristic head stripe, to remain on the whole obstinately a badger with a badger's nature. The closest these animals have come to human stylization is perhaps in the badger drawn for Kenneth Grahame's *The Wind in the Willows* by E. H. Shepard. The koala, on the other hand, has always seemed to be a natural as an alternative teddy, even when, as a marsupial, it is carrying a baby koala in its pouch, and even though it belongs to an animal group that is quite separate from the bears . Interestingly enough, the original British attempt to link Edward VII with the origin of the teddy bear concerned a koala in the London Zoo that was said to have caught Edward's attention when he was still Prince of Wales.

To stretch a point even further, there are the examples of Elisabeth Beresford's Wombles of Wimbledon Common, which enjoyed quite a vogue a few years ago in Britain. Television versions were produced of the original stories and these prompted the appearance in the shops of Womble characters, such as Great-

Uncle Bulgaria. The Wombles are burrow-dwelling animals of a genus unknown to science, though their appearance leads one to suspect there must have been a bear-cross, or perhaps a koala-cross, somewhere in their ancestry.

Reaching out towards other worlds, we stumble across the Ewoks, the diminutive bear-like intelligences who first appear in the sixth *Star Wars* movie epic, *The Return of the Jedi*. Having caught hold of the popular imagination, they made a come-back in other films of the series, and at the same time they started showing up on shop shelves alongside the more earth-bound teddies.

Before we leave the subject of adaptations, we should note the emergence of the bear as a car mascot, equipped with suckers on its paws, the better to cling to the insides of car windows. These types usually take their inspiration from the gaudy Care Bear model and seem to be a desperate attempt to cheer up the business of modern driving as they grin manically out at other vehicles. Even these creatures, we may rest assured, will pick up a measure of enchantment over time and will assume their place in the ranks of the collectable.

The process set in motion by the appearance of the earliest teddy bears is clearly by no means at an end and no doubt it has further developments in store that would have been considerable surprises to Morris Michtom and Margarete Steiff.

LITERARY BEARS

IT IS IMPORTANT to distinguish between 'bear literature' and literature that happens to contain teddy bears. The former category is by far the vaster in scope and almost all of it falls under the heading of 'children's books'. The latter category is sparse and incidental, and the enthusiast will be hard put to it to come up with any unfamiliar gems. Serious novelists, playwrights or film makers may from time to time work a teddy bear into a plot to get a sentimental, ironic or even grotesque effect, but these occasions are not worth listing in full. Literary bears, on the other hand, began to make their appearances from the earliest stages of the teddy bear craze, and the most important ones are included here.

Needless to say, any good original editions of books about bears from any period are always highly collectable items.

WINNIE THE POOH

Here is Edward Bear, coming downstairs now, bump, bump, bump, on the back of his head, behind Christopher Robin. It is, as far as he knows, the only way of coming downstairs, but sometimes he feels that there really is another way, if only he could stop bumping for a moment and think of it. And then he feels that perhaps there isn't.

We are being introduced, of course, to the most famous bear in literature, certainly in the English-speaking world, perhaps in the world at large. He is A. A. Milne's Winnie the Pooh, who, as we have already seen, existed in real life before being immortalized in the books with their drawings by E. H. Shepard. It might have been expected that these books were very

ABOVE: *Variations on a theme: 'The Teddy Bears Picnic' in the form of music sheet, record cover and bear-shaped acrylic record. Held in the London Toy and Model Museum.*

RIGHT: *Patrick and Molly Edwards's creation, Teddy Edward, in one of his first books,* Teddy Edward in the Country *(1962).*

Teddy Edward went to find a peaceful place to recover from his fright. He knew there were some fish in the stream because he saw one jumping to catch a fly.

FACING PAGE: *A Dean's Rag Book bear of the 1940s.*

English indeed – too English, with their specific upper-middle class 1920s background of nannies and nurseries, to make the transition into other languages and cultures. The assumption is clearly wrong, for the character of Pooh Bear has shown himself to be capable of transcending most such incidental considerations. Over the years, generations have been enchanted by the Pooh stories in all the languages of Europe, and he has been an outstanding success in Russian, in which language he became 'Vinni-Pukh'. Even classical scholars may read of his exploits in *Winnie Ille Pu*, the 1961 Latin version prepared by Dr Alexander Lenard.

When A. A. Milne started to set down the Pooh stories it can scarcely have crossed his mind that these were the books for which his name would be remembered long after the successful light comedies he wrote for the London stage or his humorous essays in *Punch* were forgotten. Yet the origin of it all was really quite casual and turns out to have a certain amount of mythology attached to it in the best teddy bear tradition. Christopher Robin Milne's

Farnell bear was bought from Harrods in 1920 as a first birthday present. In his autobiography, *The Enchanted Places*, Christopher Milne graphically reconstructed that first magic moment of choosing a bear:

> *A row of teddy bears sitting in a toyshop, all one size, all one price. Yet how different each is from the next. Some look gay, some look sad. Some look stand-offish, some look lovable. And one in particular, that one over there,'has a specially endearing expression. Yes, that is the one we would like, please.*

For the small boy the new bear, at that stage known as Edward, became his inseparable toy, and so the two of them began to grow up together. The other toys in the nursery were soon joining in with the games and stories, aided and abetted by Christopher's mother, Dorothy Milne, and a new name for the bear evolved from a combination of 'Winnie', after a favourite real bear at the London Zoo, and 'Pooh', which was what Christopher happened to call a swan he used to go and feed on a nearby lake.

A. A. Milne was first persuaded to write for children by Rose Fyleman, the author of a poem that contains the line, 'There are fairies at the bottom of our garden!' which is today perhaps the only memorable thing about her. She had asked Milne to contribute to a children's magazine she was starting, and he responded by beginning to turn out the verses that were in due course collected in *When We Were Very Young* and *Now We Are Six*. It has been said that the idea of writing down the Pooh stories themselves came about on an occasion when Sir Nigel Playfair, the well-known actor-manager, happened to call on the Milne household. As the illustrious visitor sat there, Christopher Robin came down from upstairs and remarked, 'What a funny man! What a funny red face!' When his parents protested at such rudeness, he explained it was not he but Pooh who had spoken.

Here was a classic case of the humanization of a stuffed toy. 'The Pooh in my arms, the Pooh sitting opposite me at the breakfast table, was the Pooh who had climbed trees in search of honey, who had got stuck in a rabbit hole, who was "a bear of no brain at all" ', wrote Christopher Milne many years later. Apart from a liking for honey, there is nothing of the bear's animal nature in the Pooh stories, and the only trace of a shadow is the rather pleasurable pang that we feel for the loss of innocence. Mary Hillier has commented that the texts come to seem weak when divorced from E. H. Shepard's drawings, but although the drawings are an integral part of the Pooh legend, this seems an unduly harsh judgement on Milne's stories. As the author and critic John Rowe Townsend has said in his study of children's literature, *Written for Children*:

> *The Pooh books consist of a series of episodes, of which the recollection remains pleasurable after a score of readings . . . Apart from any nostalgic pleasure, the adult returning to the Pooh books is bound to appreciate the sheer grace of craftsmanship. Milne was a most accomplished professional writer. He knew and accepted that he was a happy lightweight, and used to say merely that he had the good fortune to be like that. In children's as in adult literature, the lightweight of true quality is a rare and welcome phenomenon.*

It is also notable, of course, that presentations of the Pooh stories have been classic successes on radio. They were first broadcast many years ago in the BBC's 'Children's Hour' series, in which the late actor, Norman Shelley, created a memorable voice characterization for the eponymous hero. More recently they have been read by the actor and playwright Alan Bennett.

Winnie the Pooh and *The House at Pooh Corner* have taken their place in a pantheon of children's classics stretching from Lewis Carroll's *Alice in Wonderland* to Kenneth Grahame's *The Wind in the Willows* and Russell Hoban's *The Mouse and His Child*. These are all books that nurture a child's imagination but which, for a variety of reasons, retain a real, even a reinforced charm and enjoyment for adult readers. What sets the Pooh books a little aside from the others mentioned is that they do not have their darker underlying currents of dream and ambiguity, though they are magnificently far from bland. The creation of Pooh, for which a balance of credit must lie between the writer Milne and the illustrator Shepard, was so complete that those for whom it was a part of their cultural upbringing will never be able to see the Walt Disney Pooh as anything but an impostor. It would be unreasonable to expect followers of the Pooh cult to take any sort of objective view on this question.

The shadow side of the story, such as it is, mainly concerns Christopher Milne, who found that being the 'only child' Christopher Robin as well as the owner of the famous Pooh Bear was a heavy burden to carry into mature life. His mother had provided the world with a cosy impression of how it all came about:

> *We were all acting little incidents with Pooh and the nursery animals the whole time . . . we were all quite idiotic about it . . . Looking back to those days, I always see Pooh and the small boy with whom we shared them . . . with his large brown eyes and beautiful corn-coloured hair cut square.*

In 1952, Christopher wrote that he had actually seen very little of his father, who was, he claimed at that time, uneasy with children. It had been his mother who came to play in the nursery and who bore back to his father tales of everything that went on there. So far as he could remember, he had known 'nothing of the stories until they were published. Then my Nanny used to read them to me.' At a later stage, when he came to write his autobiography,

LEFT: *In* The Roosevelt Bears Abroad *(1907), the heroes meet King Edward VII in R. K. Culver's illustration.*

BELOW: *Clifford K. Berryman's famous cartoon of 1902 that set the whole teddy bear saga in motion.*

DRAWING THE LINE IN MISSISSIPPI

CLIFFORD K. BERRYMAN'S EPOCH-MAKING CARTOON NOVEMBER 10, 1902

this tone of bitter sadness was somewhat modi-fied and he recognized there had been a need in his father to return to and live through the various stages of childhood in his company. Writing *The Enchanted Places* was still an act of exorcism for him: 'Unfortunately the fictional Christopher Robin refused to die and he and his real-life namesake were not always on the best of terms.'

· · · · · · BILLY BLUEGUM · · · · · ·

Billy Bluegum is as much a folk hero in Australia as Mishka is in Russia, but whereas the Russian bear's origins belong many centuries back in oral story telling, Billy's can be precisely dated. In 1904 a weekly journal, the *Bulletin*, featured the first drawing of a town-raised koala of asser-tive personality who decides to head for the outback to take to his fellow creatures the bene-fits of civilization. The drawing was by Norman Lindsay, the author and illustrator of that slap-stick children's classic, *The Magic Pudding*. Billy

Bluegum's eccentric adventures were developed in a series of cartoons and stories over the years. It is worth noting that Lindsay's artwork shows us a humanized live koala rather than a huma-ized stuffed toy.

· · · · · · · THE ROOSEVELT · · · · · · ·
BEARS
· ·

This pair of travelling bears, Teddy-B and Teddy-G (standing for Teddy-Brown and Teddy-Gray), made their first appearance in 1905. Their stories, recounted in a robust doggerel by Sey-mour Eaton, were syndicated in newspapers across the United States and soon won them a wide following. They were to have several illus-trators, the best-known being Floyd Campbell and R. K. Culver, and four books of their adven-tures were published. These chronicled their travels from the Rocky Mountains to New York as well as abroad, and also their detective work in helping to solve mysteries involving various nur-sery rhyme characters. Again they are dressed-up feral animals rather than stuffed toys and, as Peter Bull remarks, are disturbingly like the sort of creature you might run into on an unwise trip to the woods. Nevertheless they deserve a place in the teddy bear saga since they are the first literary creations to exploit the association between Theodore Roosevelt (after whom teddy bears were named) and the Mitchtom toy. It may be that their popularity helped to attach the prefix 'teddy' to 'bear' in general usage.

· · · · · · · · · BEARS IN THE · · · · · · · · ·
LAND OF OZ

L. Frank Baum, the American author of *The Wizard of Oz* (1899), incorporated bears into his cast of fantastic characters in later volumes in

the series. This one, encountered in *The Lost Princess of Oz* (1917), is clearly an authentic teddy:

The bear was chubby as well as fuzzy; his body was even puffy, while his legs and arms seemed jointed at the knees and elbows and fastened to his body by pins or rivets. His ears were round in shape and stuck out in a comical way, while his round black eyes were bright and sparkling as beads.

He carries a pop-gun at his shoulder and, besides being stuffed with 'a very good quality of curled hair' and having a skin of 'the best plush that ever was made', he turns out to be a sentry guarding the approach to the city of Bear Centre which is ruled over by a powerful sorcerer in the person of the Big Lavender Bear.

BELOW: *Ruper Bear as motor-scooter rider: a friction-driven toy with its original box.*

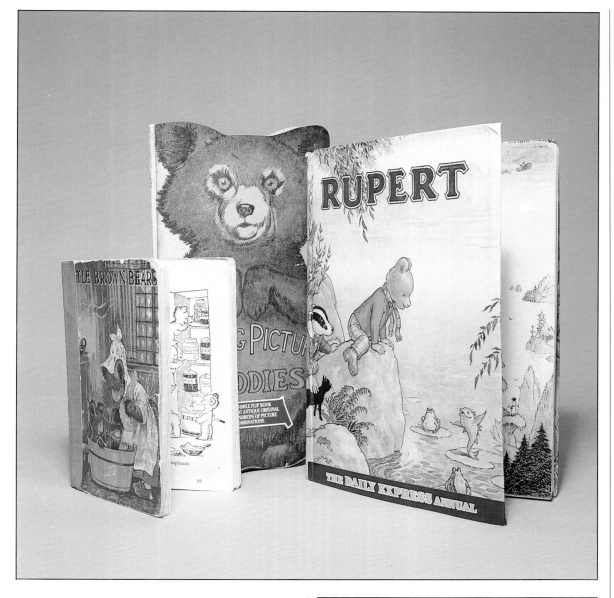

Yet another teddy features in *The Tin Woodman of Oz* (1918).

· · · · · · · RUPERT BEAR · · · · · · ·

Britain, oddly enough, was rather tardy in producing bear heroes of any stature. Before the First World War the first British story-book bear had appeared in any anonymous little publication, *The Tale of Teddy Bright-Eyes* (1909), while there had also been Harry Golding's *Tim Tubby Toes* stories (1913). Big Teddy and Little Teddy began to appear in the Josephine Books of Mrs H. C. Craddock, illustrated by Honor C. Appleton, in 1917 and continued through 12 volumes in the years that followed.

Rupert Bear, who finally caught the public imagination in a way that has endured to the present day, did not come into being until 1920.

The *Daily Express* was looking for a rival attraction to the *Daily Mail's* strip cartoon character, 'Teddy Tail'. It was Mary Tourtel, a well-known lady aviator and the wife of the newspaper's night editor, Herbert Tourtel, who came up with Rupert in the first episode of a strip-cartoon story entitled 'Little Lost Bear'. Mrs Tourtel was an accomplished illustrator, and her creation was an immediate success. She continued to draw the strip herself for 15 years, and when her eyesight began to give her trouble, handed the task on to Alfred Bestell, who was faithful to it for another 30 years. After he, in turn, decided to retire in 1965, the strip was taken over by a team of illustrators.

The adventures of Rupert and his friends, including Bill Badger and Algy the Pug, continue to appear, and the rural dream of Nutwood has moved with the times, for a visitor from outer space is now as likely as a wizard or goblin to be lurking in the hedgerows. From the beginning, the Rupert stories possessed a fetching quality of imaginative whimsy. They have been read over the years by millions of children, both in the paper and in book form in the *Rupert Annuals*. It strikes none of Rupert's fans as strange that their hero, down to his five-fingered hands, is in all respects a small boy with an animal's head.

BELOW: *A Rupert pop-up book:* Rupert and the Round Garden *(1975).*

In his alarm Raggety has left the bowl of tulips behind, and Bill takes great care of them until the chums are back in the garden. Without wasting a moment Rupert uses the Imps' spray on the flower-beds and bushes. "See, it's working!" he cries. "Yes, they look fresh and pretty now!" exclaims Gregory. "It's just like magic!" And when Daddy comes out to dig in the garden everything is so perfect that he has no idea of what has happened. "You should have seen the state of your garden a little while ago," says B as he hands Mr. Bear the bowl of tulips. "We've such a story to tell you!"

PROSPER

Besides Nounours, who featured in newspapers and comics before he became a star on television, another French bear hero of the comic strip was Prosper, invented by the cartoonist Alain Saint-Ogan for *Le Matin* in 1933. Prosper was a polar bear with spindly limbs and a perpetually annoyed expression on account of the ring and chain he carried in his nose as a relic of an unfortunate encounter with the world of men. The trend of Prosper's adventures had him making a spirited defence of himself in a world where adversity was the norm.

ABOVE: *A model of Rupert in resin, with the publication,* More Rupert Adventures.

PADDINGTON BEAR
AND OTHERS

From the 1930s onwards there was a strong tradition of nursery tales featuring bears. Gwynedd Rae's Mary Plain books (the first of which, *Mostly Mary*, was published in 1930) were still appearing in the 1950s. Biffo the Bear made his début in the *Beano* in 1948 and was also going strong in the 1950s. In addition, this was the decade which saw the first appearance on television of Andy Pandy and Teddy, and the rise to stardom of Harry Corbett's Sooty. At the same time, Joan G. Robinson began to write and publish her Teddy Robinson books, based on the real-life scrapes which this bear got into with his owner, the author's daughter Deborah. The most remarkable phenomenon of these years, however, turned out to be Michael Bond's Paddington Bear, whose adventures began in 1958 with *A Bear Called Paddington*.

Pooh may have had his origins at Harrods but Paddington's were at Selfridge's. Mr Bond, doing some last-minute shopping at Christmas 1956, spotted a forlorn bear left on its own on a shelf and bought it as a present for his wife. Within a matter of days the bear had prompted him into starting to write a story about it, and within two years the first collection of Paddington stories was in the shops, helped on its way by Peggy Fortnum's charming illustrations. Many other collections were to follow, as were a television series and what amounted to a whole Paddington industry.

Discovered on Paddington station, having mysteriously arrived there from darkest Peru, as the story tells it, with only a sun hat, a battered suitcase and a label round his neck saying, 'Please look after this bear. Thank you,' Paddington was welcomed into the Brown household as a sort of foster bear. The stories hinge on the innocent chaos he creates amid such domestic routines as shopping expeditions or family visits to the cinema. And so another generation of children took a bear to their hearts. Models of Paddington Bear, always dressed for the English

BELOW: *Paddington Bear figurines: one is a candle, another a money box and two are salt and pepper shakers.*

weather in characteristic duffle coat, sou'-wester and wellington boots, have been recorded as selling at the rate of 100,000 a year. He is not a teddy of the cuddly type, but is a reassuring personality to have around.

Since Paddington, other bears have continued to enter the literature. There are Margaret J. Baker's Shoe Shop Bears, for instance, who took their inspiration from a group of bears the author came across in a shoe shop in Devon, their task being to keep young customers

amused. There is also Peter Bull's Bully Bear, who appeared in the early 1980s and was based on the figure of the 'ideal' bear the author had helped to design for the House of Nisbet. Unfortunately, however, the Bully Bear stories

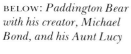

BELOW: *Paddington Bear with his creator, Michael Bond, and his Aunt Lucy*

do not seem to have the staying power of a classic, as they are weakened by archness and self-consciousness.

· · · · · · · · · · · · · · BEARS IN · · · · · · · · · · · · ·
LITERATURE
· ·

As mentioned, teddy bears make an appearance as props, motifs or decorations in literature from time to time. Dodie Smith's 1938 play *Dear*

ABOVE: *A typical Paddington Bear in teddy form.*

RIGHT: *A selection of Paddington Bear titles in first editions, with rag books and a birthday book.*

90

Octopus, for example, featured a bear called Symp whose pathos was enhanced through his having lost an arm. More recently there was a bear in Dennis Potter's novel and television series, *Blackeyes*. The bear was clung to by an aging novelist, Kingsley, in his semi-senile squalor and stolen from him as a cruel joke.

The most famous bear in literature, however, remains Aloysius in Evelyn Waugh's *Brideshead Revisited*, who is first glimpsed in the company of his aristocratic owner among the Oxford undergraduates of the 1920's.

> *I knew Sebastian by sight long before I met him. That was unavoidable for, from his first week, he was the most conspicuous man of his year by reason of his beauty, which was arresting, and his eccentricities of behaviour, which seemed to know no bounds. My first sight of him was as we passed by the door of Germer's, and, on that occasion, I was struck less by his looks than by the fact that he was carrying a large teddy bear.*
>
> *'That,' said the barber, as I took his chair, 'was Lord Sebastian Flyte. A most amusing young gentleman.'*

The narrator learns from the barber that Sebastian has just bought a hairbrush with an ivory back and very stiff bristles and was having 'Aloysius' engraved on it. This was not 'to brush him with, but to threaten him with a spanking when he was sulky'. The television series, in which Aloysius was played by one of Peter Bull's bears, helped to give this particular legend a fresh lease of life. Interestingly enough, Aloysius is said to have been based on Sir John Betjeman's bear, Archibald Ormsby-Gore, Waugh and Betjemen having been at Oxford at the same time.

Archibald features both in the late Poet Laureate's free-verse autobiography, *Summoned by Bells*, and in a story, 'Archie and the Strict Baptists'. The latter, a literary curiosity in one sense but a joy to arctophiles in another, tells us much about the character of Archie, who has a weakness for hell-fire theology and shares with his owner a delight in such period details as the patent Aneucapnic oil lamps that were used to light the Victorian interiors of nonconformist chapels. There could hardly be a better example of the balance between affectionate nostalgia and eccentric character which is so much a part of the teddy bear mystique.

BELOW: *More Paddington paraphernalia: slippers, plate and radio.*

THE BEARS OF
THE FAMOUS

LEFT: *Teddy bear with nose ring and chain, a reminder of the days of the dancing bear.*

· · · · · · · · · PETER BULL · · · · · · · · ·
· ·

THERE ARE bears of famous owners and bears who have made their owners famous. There are bears who are famous in their own right and famous hugs of bears. These form the substance of the present chapter, but no one deserves a mention in it more than the late Peter Bull, who probably did as much as anyone to contribute to the phenomenal popularity of the teddy bear in the present day. His death in 1984 at the age of 72 was a grave loss to the arctophile fraternity.

Mr Bull had briefly been a journalist before he went on the stage in the early 1930s. His thespian career was interrupted by the war, but he returned to make his mark as a forceful character actor, creating the role of Pozzo in the first London production of Samuel Beckett's *Waiting for Godot* and that of the monk Tetzel in John Osborne's *Luther*. The films in which he appeared included *Oliver Twist*, *The African Queen* and *Tom Jones*, but he is said to have grown increasingly disillusioned with an actor's

life. As an antidote, he embarked on authorship and wrote four volumes of autobiography which were acclaimed by the critic Kenneth Tynan as the most outstandingly funny set of memoirs by any actor.

In 1969 he combined his enjoyment of writing with his enthusiasm for teddy bears by publishing *Bear With Me* (called *The Teddy Bear Book* in its American edition), which turned out to be the first version of a text that would go through later stages of expansion and revision. He was frankly astonished by the response. All around the world people began to creep out of their closets in a shame-faced sort of way and to confess openly to their love of teddy bears. An extensive correspondence followed and brought Peter Bull many friends and much new material.

He was also sent bears in need of a home or care and attention, and by the end of his days his personal hug had grown to number two hundred. (These orphans found a final home in the London Toy and Model Museum at Craven Hill, which also houses the Paddington Bear archive.) The occasion that started off Peter

RIGHT: *The actress Liza Goddard's bear Sophie.*

FACING PAGE: *The novelist Barbara Cartland's bear, illustriously christened 'The Prince of Love'.*

Bull's passion for bears was when he returned from boarding school for the holidays to discover that his mother had donated his teddy bear to a sale, feeling it was appropriate for him to have outgrown such toys at the age of sixteen. It emerged that a great number of people had suffered a similar trauma through the accidental loss or deliberate destruction of a much-loved bear.

In Peter Bull's case, the bears who joined him in later years were a great consolation. Above all there was Theodore, a little two-and-a-half-inch (six centimetre) bear who became his inseparable companion on his journeys, carried in a pocket and smuggled, it will be remembered, into a meeting with President Roosevelt's daughter Alice. From his appearances on television chat shows, Theodore built up an extensive network of well-wishers and pen pals and could number such classy bears as Clarence, who belonged to the Marquess of Bath, among

his acquaintance. Peter bull claimed to be no collector, but a one-bear man at heart who had other bears thrust upon him and found it impossible to avoid the appeal of any bear in need. 'Show me a bear . . . who has been loved, beaten up, deprived of limb, eyesight or hearing and I am instantly intrigued and want to discover his history.'

Another of Peter Bull's bears to achieve fame and fortune was, of course, Delicatessen, who won the plum role of Aloysius in the television version of *Brideshead Revisited*. It was a remarkable climax to a career, the first 50 years of which had been spent immobilized on a shelf in a grocery store in Saco, Maine. When the store's owner, Miss Euphemia Ladd, retired, she presented him to Mr Bull, and when the television production team were looking for a bear of the right age and type, Delicatessen fitted the bill. As a result of his triumph he was named Aloysius.

Peter Bull's other great interest was astro-

RIGHT: *A child hugs his teddy bear.*

logy and he was part-proprietor of an astrological shop in Kensington, London, called Zodiac. For the House of Nisbet he designed, as well as the classic Bully Bear, a whole family of bears known as the Zodiac Bears who were dressed to match their astrological characters. Indeed, his last book, published only a few days before his death, was entitled *The Zodiac Bears*.

SIR JOHN BETJEMAN AND ARCHIE

It is a feature of the true arctophile to be unabashed about humanizing the thoughts and responses of teddy bears, and Peter Bull was no exception. He was glad to assist his bears, and Theodore in particular, in carrying on a correspondence and receiving letters from bears that similarly used their owners as the medium. Their most illustrious correspondent was Archibald Ormsby-Gore, who on one occasion entertained Theodore and his escort to lunch at John Betjeman's house in Cloth Fair, Smithfield. In his letters Archie was given to expressing his theological preoccupations: 'I spend much of my time thinking of the futility of mankind and the Last Judgement, when all but us Strict and Particular Baptists will be consigned to everlasting flames. I can find scriptural warrant for all of this.'

It seems likely that Archie's stern fundamentalism was a development of his old age since there is no mention of it in the childhood memory enshrined in *Summoned by Bells*. Perhaps he felt that he had a frivolous past to live down, for his name is said to have been taken from that of a character in the music halls.

In the late Poet-Laureate's verse autobiography, Archie's function is a pure benevolent humanity:

Safe were those evenings in the pre-war world
When firelight shone on green linoleum;
I heard the church bells hollowing out the sky,
Deep beyond deep, like never ending stars,
And turned to Archibald, my safe old bear,
Whose woollen eyes looked sad or glad at me,
Whose ample forehead I could wet with tears,
Whose half moon eyes received my confidence,
Who made me laugh, who never let me down.

These lines have become something of a key text in the whole mythology of the teddy bear cult. As Peter Bull remarked, '"Whose woollen eyes look sad or glad at me." That's it, isn't it, really?' And, of course, this entry of the faithful teddy bear into immortal verse is a rare departure. All too often the teddy is called upon as a representative of sentimentality; its role as friend and comforter is frequently forgotten.

· · · · · · A FEW FAMOUS HUGS · · · · · ·

Perhaps the most senior hug of bears in existence is that of Lieutenant-Colonel Robert Henderson of Edinburgh. It numbers over a hundred teddy bears and is associated with a large and distinguished collection of bear paraphernalia.

The senior bear of the hug is Teddy Boy, subsequently renamed Teddy Girl when passed down to the colonel's daughter Cynthia and dressed in a frilly skirt. This bear is an authentic 1903 model, originally the property of the colonel's elder brother and just a year older than the colonel himself. Teddy Girl indeed has a claim to being the most senior teddy bear in Britain.

'Colonel Bob', as he is known with affection in arctophile circles, has been for many years a leading evangelist for the beneficent influence of teddy bears in human lives. He was closely associated with Jim Ownby in promoting the Good Bears of the World movement and was responsible for setting up its United Kingdom branch. He has also done much to develop what may be called the philosophy of the modern bear cult, relating it back to its archetypal appeal.

In the autumn 1977 issue of *Bear Tracks*, the magazine of the Good Bears of the World Association, he wrote:

From early times the bear has commanded a special place in folklore, myth, fairy-tale and legend. It has been regarded as representative of both divine and natural forces; and today, in the form of the Teddy Bear, it is grasped in psychic compensation and clung to for security. The reason for this is that the bear functions as a powerful symbol that provides satisfaction for a widespread psychological need. Consequently, history, religion, philosophy and psychology are all involved in any proper explanation of the mystique of the Teddy Bear.

ABOVE: *A Schuco page-boy bear: highly restored, this 'Yes/No' bear was made in the 1920s and is the property of Judy Sparrow.*

For record-breaking bear collections in terms of numbers, however, we must look to the United States, the man at the top of this particular league being Matt Murphy, a banker who lives in Texas and whose collection is reported to consist of upwards of 1,300 bears, though this figure also includes his many pieces of paraphernalia. Mr Murphy has built up his collection with examples from 135 countries. In Flushing, Michigan, there lives James Walt, who is known to his friends as the 'Teddy Baron' for his hug of more than 250 teddy bears, which may well be the largest collection to consist entirely of true teddies. Other contenders may in the course of time be making a bid for a place in the record books. Virginia Walker of Florida, for instance, has named her house Teddy Towers to celebrate its ever-increasing numbers of inmates, reported recently to consist of over 600 bears of all types.

LEFT: *'Teddy's New Tin Drum', a model by Haphenricksen – a limited edition made in 1983.*

FACING PAGE: *Bears on a homemade roundabout, and a jack-in-the-box bear.*

An especially attractive hug is that of Mrs Patricia Fitt of Hamden in Connecticut: a working community of 74 miniature bears, none of which is taller than four inches (10 cms). They live in a part of the house called the Bear House Workshop where they have rooms for every activity and recreation, including a school room, a carpenter's shop and a library as well as living rooms and bathrooms. In Britain, the Wareham Bears of Wareham in Dorset are a comparable hug of a hundred or so bears in domestic and working surroundings who are on exhibition to the public outside the winter months.

ACTION BEARS AND MASCOTS

There are many examples of bears who travel widely or who go mountaineering or parachute or sky dive or become involved as stalwart mascots in hazardous circumstances. Colonel Henderson, for instance, kept a miniature teddy with him throughout his Second World War service, including the time he spent on Montgomery's staff in Europe. There was a bear called Zissi who climbed the North Face of the Matterhorn in 1965 and reputedly encouraged

ABOVE: *The* Observer *magazine cover for 28 July 1985, which reproduced a famous pre-war* Picture Post *cover showing the Queen Mother with a bear when she was Duchess of York.*

his partner, Walter Bonatti, to press on for the summit when all seemed lost. But the most famous heroic mascot is probably Donald Campbell's Mr Woppit. He was with his owner on all his record-breaking attempts on land and water speed records, survived the crash on Coniston Water in 1967 in which Campbell died and is today owned by his daughter, Gina Campbell, who carries on with the family tradition of challenging speed records. The bear is a common mascot, of course, in sports circles, Montreal Ted, who marched at the head of the British team in Montreal in the 1976 Olympic Games, being one example.

The most travelled bear in the world is Teddy Edward, whose journeys have ranged from the Himalayas to the Sahara, up the Niger River and across the United States. His travels, starting in 1962, have been documented in photographs by Patrick Matthews and written up by Patrick's wife Mollie, and they are chronicled in books and children's television programmes. The original Teddy Edward in fact became somewhat travel-worn and weary and stepped aside for a successor, who underwent a little

plastic surgery to make him into an exact replica.

As we might expect, the teddy bear mascot is far from uncommon in the world of show-business where good luck is ever an important commodity. Among singers, the late Elvis Presley had kept a bear by him since childhood, and from the moment his song 'I Just Want to be Your Teddy Bear' was recorded he received an avalanche of bears and bear bric-à-brac in the post. Another singer who has owned to having a teddy is Dusty Springfield, whose bear is called Einstein, and bears have been mentioned in connection with the names of Dame Margot Fonteyn, Nadia Nerina, Dustin Hoffman, Jill Bennett, Lynn Redgrave and Samantha Eggar.

· · · · · · · BEAR OCCASIONS · · · · · · ·

Famous bears and famous people with their bears are often known to lend support to good causes by means of teddy bear gatherings, picnics and competitions. These jamborees, on the one hand, provide excuses for arctophiles to indulge their passion, but on the other they are frequently harnessed to the most worthy fund-raising causes. The legendary 'Great Teddy Bear Rally and Honey Fair' of 8,000 bears at Longleat on 27 May 1979, sponsored by the Marquess of Bath and his bear Clarence in association with the Good Bears of the World movement, was in aid of Dr Barnardo's Homes. The Good Bears of the World have also instituted 27 October each year as 'Good Bear Day', that day being President Roosevelt's birthday.

The year 1976 saw several celebrations of Winnie the Pooh's 50th birthday in his home county of Kent. For the first of these, in June, the original Pooh was flown over from New York (he lived at the time in the offices of E. P. Dutton, the American publishers of the Pooh books, though today his address is care of the Central Children's Room in New York Public Library). Methuen, the British publishers, set up their celebration on 14 October, complete with wine, a picnic and games of Pooh sticks, though Pooh himself was absent since he had another party to attend at the Bronx Zoo. This date was settled on as being the anniversary of the first publication of *Winnie the Pooh*, but Christopher Milne declined to attend. He protested, with some justification, that Pooh was

really 55 at the time, for his actual birthday ought to be reckoned from the day he was bought at Harrods.

Bear events and occasions continue to be immensely popular all around the world, from America to Australia and New Zealand. At one point Colonel Henderson issued a set of guidelines on how to organize a teddy bear competition. These are notable for their military preci-

sion and they cover such vital points as safeguarding, exhibiting and classifying bears for the judging as well as ensuring that they are afterwards returned to their rightful owners. The colonel's advice will surely come into its own in the teddy bear centenary year of 2003, which, we may be sure, will witness more junketings and jubilees than the bear world has ever seen before.

ASSOCIATED BEAR
PARAPHERNALIA

BEAR BRIC-À-BRAC AND OTHER ITEMS

IT SOMETIMES seems as if there is no limit to the range of paraphernalia and bric-à-brac that utilizes the bear motif. Teddy bear collectors often extend their interest enthusiastically in this direction even though a certain amount of the material may be more akin to the wild bear than to the teddy. Perhaps this is the newest phase of the bear cult. The number of objects concerned are legion and it would be impossible to set down a comprehensive list of them. There are many examples which may be clearly linked with the teddy bear craze, but others precede it or are quite unconnected with it.

We have mentioned earlier the bear musical boxes and automata as well as bear toys of the type sometimes known as 'jumping jacks'. Apart from these there are such functional items as bears that serve as umbrella stands (Colonel Henderson has one in his collection and Pam Hebbs illustrates another). Bears have been used as motifs for ink wells, corkscrews, condiment sets, porcelain town souvenirs, table lighters, chess pieces, scraps and book ends. Collectors who keep their eyes open will be surprised by what they may come across in antique or bygone shops, junk stalls or church bazaars, but 'bargains' are few and far between. Dealers are these days well aware of the fact that anything remotely to do with bears will quickly catch the eye of an enthusiast and be snapped up. Any item made of hand-carved wood will always have a special value.

From the moment when teddy bear fever first set in, a plethora of products began to exploit the new popular image. There were nursery china and tea sets illustrated with bears. Ivory teething rings with silver teddies attached to them became popular as christening presents. There were also lockets, charms, cuff-links, thimbles, brooches, badges and trinkets as well as a variety of board and card games and puzzles, not to mention teddy bear muffs. As early as 1907, the *Boston Sunday Globe* featured

LEFT: *A teddy bear metamorphosed into a nursery clock.*

ABOVE: *Bears as, respectively, a teapot, a honey pot, and a pair of salt and pepper shakers.*

a series of teddy cut-out dolls with changes of clothes, and other magazines and journals followed. Often inventive and charming, and drawn by leading graphic artists, the cut-out teddy has been with us ever since.

Meanwhile the list of objects associated with teddies has never ceased to expand. There have been teddy bear purses, nightdress cases and hot-water bottle covers, or even rubber hot-water bottles themselves in the shapes of bears.

There have been cake decorations and Christmas-tree ornaments, clocks, cookie jars and, of course, honey pots. Models of bears in plastic or porcelain are always obtainable, and it is worth keeping an eye open for well-designed examples. Indeed, the whole area of teddy bear ephemera commends itself to the collector, since prices can be expected to rise.

It is a general rule of the times we live in that yesterday's ephemera is swiftly transformed

104

into today's collectables, and postcards and greetings cards are a case in point. By the time the teddy bear was invented, the vogue for sending postcards was at its height, helped on its way by new colour-printing techniques and the decision of the British Post Office in 1894 to bring in a special halfpenny rate for post-cards. The teddy vogue at once joined forces with the postcard vogue, and teddy cards have been produced ever since.

The collectors of general novelty and humorous cards are in direct rivalry for these items with the collectors of teddy paraphernalia. This means that the best examples and sets of series, usually showing scenes from the family lives of bears, keep increasing in value. The social history reflected in the messages on the backs of the cards is also of interest for collec-tors, especially if the messages go beyond the routine, 'Thought you would like this for your

ABOVE: *A bear that doubles as a purse. It is German, c 1913, has jointed limbs, and its blond plush is unusual.*

105

album', or 'Wish you were here.' The cards themselves are valuable for bear historians, as they can usually be dated from postmarks or catalogues and they illustrate the evolving features of the fashions in bears. The photographic cards, often used for birthday greetings in the 1920s and 1930s especially, illustrate fine examples of all kinds and makes of bear in prime condition. Any postcard, greeting or Christmas card that has a bear as part of its design is grist to the mill of the arctophile collector, and any modern examples can simply be salted away until their time comes round, which is sure to happen quickly enough.

In the early days, many songs and music pieces on the theme of bears were published for use in theatres or music halls or simply for Saturday-evening entertainments round the piano in the parlour. The music John W. Bratton wrote for 'The Teddy Bears Picnic' in 1907 was one example. As Peter Bull has pointed out, 'between 1907 and 1911 over 40 titles beginning with the words "Teddy" or "Teddy Bear" were registered for copyright purposes', and

heaven only knew how many others there must have been. There were teddy bear marches, cake walks, rags, boogies, waltzes, balls and frolics. There were jungle teddies and home teddies and songs to welcome teddies back when they had been away or lullabies to sing to them at bedtime. Teddies danced, sang, played games, took off in airships and had picnics. The published music sheets, however obscure, undistinguished or forgotten the piece, are prized items for collectors, the entertaining lithographic covers often being the best things about them.

'The Teddy Bears Picnic' is another matter altogether. In its musical form it enjoyed a period of popularity as a piece for bands and light orchestras, but then dropped into the background. In 1930 the London music publisher Bert Feldman suggested to a rising young songwriter called James Kennedy that he write some lyrics to go with it. Mr Kennedy obliged and the song in its new version was incorporated into a pantomime in Manchester, England. Not long after this, in 1932, the band leader Henry

ABOVE: *A glass bear, two silver bear cruets and various pottery bears, including a candlestick.*

FACING PAGE: *A teddy bear muff for a little girl, made by Merrythought in the 1960s.*

TOP: *A bear nutcracker, and a bear ashtray and matchbox holder, both German, carved in the Black Forest in the 1920s.*

ABOVE: *Selection of badges and buttons featuring bears as their motifs.*

Hall was appointed to take over the BBC Dance Orchestra and began to look for a wider range of material, including some children's numbers. They re-orchestrated 'The Teddy Bears Picnic' to give it a try in a broadcast and the response was sensational. Letters and requests for repeats poured into Broadcasting House, and Henry Hall lost no time in issuing his own so-called 'novelty' record with the lyrics sung by Val Rosing. This best-selling disc had been continually available in one form or another by the time Henry Hall died at the age of 91 in 1989, and its sales were reputed to have run to several million.

Collecting recordings of songs connected with teddy bears may be a little more specialized than collecting the other items mentioned in this chapter, but the records are certainly to be found. They range from the rather irritating nursery jingle, 'Me and My Teddy Bear' ('have no worries, have no care!') to Elvis Presley's 'Let Me Be Your Teddy Bear'. In his *Film Companion*, Leslie Halliwell dismisses the 1957 movie *Loving You* as an 'Empty-headed, glossy star vehicle.' This was the film, however, which introduced that particular song. Confirmed bear enthusiasts will therefore largely overlook its faults, even as they forgive the song for being hardly one of Elvis's best. It has been released and reissued on various Elvis Presley albums since 1957. Early pressings in good shape are the ones the serious collector will try to find.

WELL-CONNECTED PARAPHERNALIA

Increasingly in recent years we have seen ranges of incidental products coming on to the market to celebrate some bear personality who happens for the moment to be a media star. These may be directly linked with the promotion accompanying the release of a film or a new television series or book. Alternatively, the reproduction rights may be licensed by the copyright holder to a manufacturer of various lines who wishes

to exploit a particular image. The types of object are again immensely diverse. If we mention wallpapers and fabrics, oven gloves, lavender bags, aprons and shopping bags, pyjamas, nighties and boxer shorts, we are still only scratching the surface.

The process goes back at least to Winnie the Pooh, who was responsible for inspiring a whole range of products. These have included over the years, as Peter Bull chronicles, Christopher Robin classroom readers, calendars, birthday books, get-well books, notepaper and smocks. On top of those there have been Pooh nursery

ABOVE: *A bear cigarette lighter, a celluloid bear with cubs, a silver bear with bone teething ring, and a Swiss bear key ring.*

109

RIGHT: *A teddy bear, the property of Barbara and Beneta Brown, finds his style with badges, tie and bracelet.*

prints, Christmas and birthday cards, pop-up books, garden figures, T-shirts, silver honey spoons and, more recently, pocket calculators. The moment the Walt Disney films came along with their variant Pooh figure, the entire process was set in motion afresh.

It was reported from France that the appearance of Nonours on television prompted an avalanche of products, including 800,000 records and seven million postcards, quite apart from the boost he gave to the sales of teddy bears in general. In Britain Paddington Bear has had a similar impact and the rights sales to use his name on more than 200 products have reportedly made him the world's highest-paid bear. As well as Paddington T-shirts, stickers, chocolates and a 'Paddington Anywhen Marmalade', there has also been a Paddington computer game. In 1983, he even had a hit in the charts with a single, 'Cross My Paws and Hope to Die', extrac-

ted from a best-selling record, *Paddington Bear's Magical Musical*. Other numbers on this disc included 'Everlasting Toffee', 'Marmalade 'n Me' and 'Bearobics'.

THE BEAR ACCESSORIES

Accessories for bears can be hard to distinguish from accessories for any other kind of stuffed toy or doll since dolls' clothes and even outgrown items of children's dress may readily be utilized for a bear's wardrobe. Vintage bears which were originally sold with clothes and which still have their costumes or wardrobes with them naturally tend to be rare and valuable. Outfits for bears, including hats, sets of underclothes and all kinds of outdoor and fancy dress, began to be manufactured at a very early stage of the

LEFT: *R. & R. Hill's distinctive Antique Bear Collection consists of a set of six bears made of resin.*

BELOW: **Ready Teddy Go,** *a fold-out bear story, bear travel accessories (bag, purse and handkerchief) and a cut-out bear.*

teddy craze. Cut-out clothes and knitting patterns were plentiful.

It even became possible to buy specially made teddy furniture, including chairs, tables and baths, as well as carriages and motor cars for them to ride out and about in. There were circus cages and wagons for those who felt the teddy bear still needed a measure of restraint. These, presumably, were the same people who bought them leads, collars and muzzles. Meanwhile miniature bears could make themselves look contentedly settled amid the domestic setting of standard dolls' house furnishings.

As Pam Hebbs points out, it is always worth some trouble to the arctophile to keep an eye open for miniature travellers' samples of hats, briefcases, gloves and other items to enhance the stylishness of a favourite bear. Meanwhile there is a lot of fun to be had from spotting the imaginative possibilities of an old pair of spec-

RIGHT: *The way an odd item of dress can enhance a bear's personality is shown here.*

FACING PAGE: *Sweatshirt, cravat and striped pants give a well-worn bear a renewed self-esteem.*

tacles, motoring goggles, watch chain or similar junk-shop item.

· · · · · · · · · · · BEARS IN · · · · · · · · · ·
ADVERTISING
· ·

The powerfully reassuring figure of the teddy bear has been used repeatedly by advertisers over the years. Items of advertising ephemera which feature bears are consequently as collectable as anything else that links up with the bear cult. Bears were the trade mark and trade name of the French corsetières, Buscs à l'Ours. A well-known advertisement, dating from 1882 and so preceding the teddy bear, shows lady bears being fitted with corsets in one of the company's shops. The firm of Bear Brand Stockings, with its headquarters in Chicago, had at one time rather oddly used a grizzly bear as a trade mark. When nylon stockings came in, they decided to opt for an altogether more suave image and chose 'Chad', a Chad Valley bear with top hat and cane to advertise their product in shops and stores. In due course one of the original Chads was sold at Sotheby's for an appropriately handsome sum. Any Bear Brand advertising

material is collectable and much sought after.

A teddy bear mascot was also the symbol of Peak Frean biscuits and was used in their advertising for the best part of 60 years from shortly before the First World War. The Peak Frean delivery vans, with three-foot-high (one metre) bears riding on their roofs , were a feature of the London streets over a long period. A bear called 'Cosy' was at a later stage the centrepiece for a 1960s campaign in Britain to promote solid coal as a source of domestic heating. Sponsored by the National Coal Board as a part of their Coal Utilization Campaign, clones of Cosy were to be seen sitting in innumerable coal merchants' windows.

Other examples of bears used in advertising include one adopted by the Bank of Montreal, which significantly has, as president of its Californian branch, Mr Matt Murphy, the proprietor of the world's largest hug. The advertisement shows a teddy lying in a safe-deposit box with the caption, 'What to do with your valuables'. An especially fine advertisement for 'Eveready' flashlights and batteries showed a small boy on the stairs at night, clutching a torch whose beam struck the teddy bear he held for comfort and projected its shadow as a live bear on the wall

above him. This eloquently expressed a sense of the ambivalence of both bears and darkness, and it backed up its message with a well-chosen quotation from Shakespeare's *Richard III:*

> *. . . shadows tonight*
> *Have struck more terror to the soul of Richard*
> *Than can the substance of ten thousand soldiers.*

Other examples abound. British Rail used a drawing of a little girl holding a bear to promote its Family Railcard fare-saving scheme, and Pan American Airlines invented the figure of Pierre Panda to be used on pamphlets and booklets for distribution to children who were passengers on their flights. Pierre Panda was therefore a character whose function was a deliberately reassuring one in an age when more and more families are undertaking international journeys by air. Further examples from every period come to light on sweet and biscuit tins and all sorts of wrappings, and any present-day examples are worth hoarding away for the future. The magpie instinct of the collector with an eye for good specimens will invariably pay off in the long run.

Actual bears have on occasion been given away as incentives in promotion campaigns and any bear that may be linked to such an event will obviously have a little snippet of interest of its own. In the meantime, it is always in the collector's interest to watch out for old illustrated catalogues like those issued by manufacturers or distributed by shops and stores before Christmas. These often contain precise information on dating styles and innovations which may not be readily available elsewhere. Their study is also important for developing a background knowledge of how the teddy bear has continued in its evolution.

Finally, we should mention those bears which have played a role in altruistic rather than commercial causes. There is the large bear sporting two tones of grey, for instance, which is the impressive mascot figure of the Royal National Lifeboat Institution in Britain. But the most famous of all such bears must surely be Smokey Bear, the eminently practical spirit behind the

ABOVE: *The Standard Sewing Machine Company used a bear as their company motif.*

FACING PAGE: *Two miniature bears with a doll's* chaise longue; *the seat was made for Queen Victoria as a child.*

ABOVE: *Four Victorian magic-lantern slides from a set telling the story of 'Goldilocks and the Three Bears'.*

FACING PAGE: *Teddy bear with basket, in prime condition.*

US Department of Agriculture's campaign to counter the threat of forest fires. It is rumoured that Smokey was adopted as a symbol of the campaign way back in 1902 as yet another product of the publicity attending President Roosevelt's refusal to shoot that little brown bear in Michigan.

Smokey has gone from strength to strength, especially since 1953 when the Ideal Toy Company, led at the time by Maurice Michtom's son Benjamin, obtained from the US Government the exclusive rights to manufacture Smokey as a toy. This concession was based on the ingenious idea of making every child purchaser of the toy an honorary Junior Forest Ranger, who would then receive from the Department of Agriculture an official badge and an action pack of information on the elementary precautions that need to be taken against fires in forest lands. The American traveller, if so inclined, will have the opportunity of picking up car stickers and posters featuring Smokey Bear when on visits to the national parks there, and will also find the hero featured in various books and comics.

8

WHAT TO LOOK FOR
IN A BEAR

LEFT: *The profile of this teddy bear highlights his stitched nose and worn muzzle.*

THE GENERAL APPROACH

WHO GOES out and buys a bear? Parents do, of course. It is a most important matter, buying a bear by proxy for any infant, of whose life it will be a part for a long time to come. The basic fact of buying a bear shows an instinctive wish for the child to enjoy, as it grows, a fundamental sense of safety and security in its home background. The sort of teddy bear chosen in the meantime reveals as much about the psychology of the purchaser as does the choice of a certain breed or personality of dog. There never was such a wide range of bears available in stores and toy shops as there is today. All kinds of cultural and economic influences may come into play in deciding which to choose.

Such bears are, of course, bound for the hurly-burly of domestic life and are likely to find themselves in the thick of it. How many of them will survive to make vintage bears themselves in 50 years' time is anybody's guess. Whatever becomes of them, they will have served their cause well and will depart the scene honourably if they have simply been well-loved.

The motives of adults who buy bears for themselves may be different from or similar to those involved in buying bears for children. Many a hug of bears has its origin in one particular brand-new or well-worn bear that suddenly touched the heart-strings and prompted an impulse to buy. It may well be that there are people around today who would buy a bear purely for what they hope will be its rising value as an investment, but somehow, one feels, any self-respecting bear would find a subtle way of melting such stoney-hearted calculation. The reason discovered by Peter Bull to be more common than could possibly be imagined for buying a bear was to compensate for having suffered the loss of a bear in earlier years. This could be through accident, theft or the actions of well-meaning but over-anxious parents who decide that the time has arrived for Bears To Be Grown Out Of.

The development that has drawn the arctophile into the ranks of serious collectors is, however, a relatively recent one. A hobby that was

119

RIGHT: *Three bears representing the different sizes to be found.*

FACING PAGE: *An English bear of 1912, showing the gradual modification of the classic features.*

probably regarded before as a harmless eccentricity has earned respect and even taken on more than a touch of glamour through the high prices now being fetched for certain vintage bears in the sale rooms. As a consequence, the arctophile needs to become less of a happy-go-lucky amateur and more of a precisely informed specialist. There is a certain mystique attached to the world of the dealers, but well-informed amateur enthusiasts can always hold their own provided they do their homework.

The history of bears meanwhile continues to unfold and continues to have its obscure corners.

The first task facing the would-be collector is to get to know the signs, qualities and other pointers which indicate that a bear is of a certain make or period, as well as to know what makes some types rarer and hence more sought after than others. After that the would-be-collector must decide whether to remain a generalist, gathering together bears of all periods on a basis of personal response; or whether to specialize in, say, miniature bears or musical-box bears or even perhaps those ursine aristocrats, the teddies manufactured 50 or more years ago by the firm of Steiff. In fact the opportunities for

RIGHT: *A German bear, c 1910, with long arms, tapered ankles and flat feet.*

ABOVE: *The profile of the 1910 German bear shown above.*

specialization, too, have never been wider than they are today. Any individual collector will be governed by his or her own temperament, but a nice mix is probably the most attractive option.

· · · · · · GETTING TO KNOW · · · · ·
YOUR BEARS

From all that has been said it follows that self-education should be seriously considered, but, given the nature of the subject, the process should be kept enjoyable. Your simple objective is to be able to judge what it is you are looking at. In a thoroughly relaxed way, you can start to do this through illustrated books on teddies (of which you are soon bound to start building up a small library). The present interest in recent social history has led to an increase in the number of museums of toys and childhood. There are now several museums devoted entirely to teddy bears. It will be well worth the trouble to

visit as many of these establishments as you possibly can. The museums often publish excellent information packs or catalogues of their own collections. They also have archives, and researchers interested in teddy bear scholarship can apply to see them.

You should keep an eye on your local auction houses' announcements for any sales of dolls and bears. Collections of auctioneers' catalogues can build up into useful sources of information, especially if you have attended the auction yourself and been able to note down a record of prices fetched in the margin. Major auction rooms such as Sotheby's and Christies in London, of course, mainly take on the most rare and extravagant bears at the top end of the market. If you are actually buying, then there are advantages in visiting provincial sale rooms as prices will be lower there and the range of bears coming under the hammer will be wider and less predictable. Catalogue descriptions, however, may not be so reliable since local firms will not, like the metropolitan auction houses, have their own teddy bear expert. Keep it in mind that, generally speaking, the onus of responsibility is on bidders at auctions to satisfy themselves that the object being sold is genuinely what the auctioneer claims it to be.

The market in bears, as we have said, has been deliberately created, whether or not we like to think of it in this way. The market price of any period bear is defined in the auction rooms, and these prices always tend to rise. If you manage to buy the bear your heart most desires at an auction, remember that you will be obtaining it nott at a 'bargain' price but at the price that is current for that level of the market. You may even be paying rather more than that if you get carried away in the bidding, as is quite likely when it comes to bears. Remember, too, that many auction houses today impose the so-called buyer's premium of ten per cent on top of whatever a bid happens to reach. Strictly speaking you should always go into an auction with a clear idea of what you ought to be paying, or can afford to pay, for a certain bear, and be disciplined enough to drop out of the bidding if it rises beyond your limit. This is how the dealers function, but then their living depends on judging what they can charge in shops or other outlets to show a margin of profit.

Some people are daunted by the idea of attending an auction if they have never been to one before. If you feel nervous about the prospect, then go along to one or two appropriate auctions, just to sit in on them and quietly observe how they work. You will soon pick up the gist of the process. It is a myth that blinking an eye at the wrong moment may land you with an item you never wanted. You will notice that all the dealers and buyers have their own bidding manner. If you are seriously intending to bid, then study the auctioneers' conditions of sale carefully. These will be printed in the catalogue. A banker's reference may be required for bids over a certain amount. It is also a good idea to introduce yourself to the auctioneer before the bidding starts, especially if he does not know you.

These days prices tend to go out of date very quickly. It is therefore up to you to keep abreast of the main trends. In Britain, the *Lyle Official Antiques Review*, an annual publication, usually shows a selection of teddy bears, with prices, auctioned in the previous year, and the

ABOVE: *A typical English bear of the 1930s, sporting a green silk scarf.*

LEFT: *The same bear in profile, with the scarf removed to show the neck joint.*

ABOVE RIGHT: *A profile shot of the 'Little Charmer' bear seen on page 118.*

BELOW RIGHT AND OPPOSITE: *This Chad Valley bear of the 1930s shows both the Aerolite button in the right ear and the rounding and softening of the muzzle and general body outline in this period.*

same firm's companion volume in its *Antiques and Their Values Series: Dolls and Toys*, is also reissued regularly in an updated edition. Apart from this, you can ask for price lists from specialist sales and watch the press, who will always make much of any outrageous price achieved. From time to time, toy and bear fairs are arranged and provide opportunities to buy or sell, look and chat and generally keep up to date. The specialist vintage toy and teddy shops also give clear indications of price trends by what they feel able to charge to collectors. Remember, however, that their prices may well reflect some costs for repair or restoration. (Assessing the condition of a bear, and its repairability, are covered in the next chapter.)

The advantages of buying at bear or toy fairs or in specialist shops are, of course, the range of types of bear from many periods that you will find to choose from as well as the chance of a surprise discovery that may irresistibly fill a gap in your collection or set you going in an entirely fresh direction. As far as price trends are concerned, the Steiff bears remain the star attractions of the sale rooms, but it is noticeable that British bears from 50 or so years ago, like those made by Farnell, Chad Valley or Merrythought, have begun to rise in the price league, indicating a growing interest among collectors.

IDENTIFICATION

From the earliest days of the teddy bear craze there was a proliferation of manufacturers, many of whom came and went and whose names fell into oblivion. There are also manufacturers who are known from advertisements or other commercial ephemera or records but examples of whose bears have never been positively identified. Originally the great majority of teddies must have come with a tag, a trade label or token, such as the Steiff ear-button, but it is quite a rare event for these to survive in company with the bear. Many must have been discarded when the bear was first bought, and it would have been most unlikely for the original owner to have sewn an accidentally attached label back on again.

The linked questions of authentication and identification are therefore not always easy ones. Would-be collectors must keep many aspects in mind as they develop an eye for summing up a bear. They certainly need to be familiar with the evolution of the typical teddy bear profile over the course of its history. They also need to absorb as much knowledge as possible of the leading teddy bear manufacturers and what the main individual characteristics of their products have been at various times. If they are collecting recent as distinct from vintage bears, then they should also be *au fait* with technical developments in materials and manufacturing techniques. The very first all-washable 'safe eye' bear was introduced in the 1950s, for instance, by Wendy Boston Playsafe Toys. With recent bears, of course, the documentation becomes altogether more reliable and accessible.

The whole area of teddy scholarship has its vagueness and contradictions, and there is scope for anyone to research the original records and emerge with some hard facts. Judging a bear's age or identifying its make depends mainly on experience and common sense. The use of

traditional materials in fact changes relatively seldom. From the 1920s onwards, for instance, kapok often replaced wood wool as stuffing in British bears. Synthetic fur materials or plastic eyes will usually indicate a post-Second World War bear, but natural materials are still often used to make the best quality bears.

In Britain, the system of numbering designs registered with the Patent Office can be a useful researcher's tool for tracing makers and dates, though this is mostly relevant to bear-associated objects like china or novelty items such as pyjama cases.

SOME LEADING MAKERS OF BEARS

The Profile of the 'classic bear' from which all later developments spring has been described in Chapter Two. The following are among the most important firms to have contributed to that history (in order of their founding):

J. K. FARNELL Farnell's were one of the most senior family firms to specialize in the manufacture of stuffed toys, having been in business since 1840. They operated as a sort of family cottage industry in Acton, west London, until their Alpha Works factory was built adjacent to the family house at the end of the First World War. It is said to have been a Farnell 'Alpha' bear that Dorothy Milne bought for her little son Christopher at Harrods. Farnell's had started out by making toy animals from rabbit skins, but they also seem to have been pioneers in the use of Yorkshire plush fabric for stuffed animals. There are indications (never finally proven) of a link between Farnell's and Steiff when it came to originating the plush bear. Certainly the Farnell bears were very close to the Steiff pattern. The business was closed down in 1934 after a terrible fire had swept through the Farnell house and put the factory out of operation, but one of their former directors, J. C. Janisch, had by that stage already founded the Shropshire firm of Merrythought (see below).

STEIFF COMPANY The year 1880 is the official foundation date for Steiff, though Margarete Steiff had been carrying on her small business from home for several years previously. The importance of being familiar with Steiff bears,

the way their body shapes have evolved since 1903 and the various shades and types of plush that have been used in making them, can hardly be over-emphasized. They are the standard against which all other bears may ultimately be judged, being both highly individual and influential. The expert will always be able to identify a Steiff original, whether or not it has its ear-button. Steiff buttons and labels, where they do survive on a bear, convey a good deal of coded information on date, type and materials used. The Steiff museum at Giengen is a place of wonder and pilgrimage for all arctophiles.

CHAD VALLEY Although this company had its origins with a printing works in the 1820s, the key date in its history is 1897, the year in which it moved into new premises in the valley of the river Chad on the south-west outskirts of Birmingham. It was not until the First World War, however, that it began to manufacture dolls and soft toys, taking advantage of the gap in the market created by the blocking of German imports. The trade name of 'Chad Valley' was adopted in 1919, and their own line in teddy bears began to be manufactured from about 1920 onwards in a range of sizes and qualities. The earliest Chad Valley bears bore a metal trade button, usually though not invariably clipped to the ear, that carried the legend 'Chad Valley British Hygienic Toys'. They also had a label stitched underneath one foot. The labels, which have gone through a number of variations in wording over the years, are the main indicators to authenticate a Chad Valley bear. Chad Valley were the makers of the commercial version of Harry Corbett's Sooty.

IDEAL TOY COMPANY This is the senior firm of all American manufacturers of teddy bears, being the descendant of the Ideal Novelty and Toy Company, set up after 1903 to capitalize on the instant success of Maurice Mitchtom's original 'Teddy's bear'. There are unfortunately some quite considerable problems in identifying Ideal bears, owing to the fact that there never seems to have been a company policy to tag or label their teddies. Ideal bears tend to look, in fact, very like Steiff bears, though the experienced assessor will be aware of small differences of detail. For example, the ears tend to be large and set fairly low on the head, and the feet to be slightly pointed.

127

FACING PAGE: *These two Merrythought bears both date from the 1930s, but are very different in type, as their profiles (RIGHT AND FAR RIGHT) also demonstrate. The one sitting down has a button on his left shoulder which may be clearly seen in his profile portrait.*

DEAN'S Dean's Rag Book Company Ltd, founded in the south London borough of Merton in 1903, is today Britain's oldest surviving manufacturer of teddy bears. Among its other toys and products, the company has continued to produce a fine line of teddies based on vintage designs.

HERMANN After Steiff, Hermann is the best-known manufacturer of teddies, having been founded in 1907 specifically to make bears. An early Hermann bear is a rare animal and hard to distinguish from a Steiff. Later on another branch of the company included all kinds of other sorts of doll among its products. The present-day Hermann range includes traditional 'nostalgic' bears, 'No-No' bears (which were like the 'Yes-No' bears but only turned their heads from side to side and a musical box bear which plays 'The Teddy Bears Picnic'.

SCHREYER & CO. This Nuremberg company, formed in 1912, was responsible for the famous Schuco miniature bears, the 'Yes/No' bear and clockwork bears of various abilities. Its history has been outlined in Chapter Three, as has that of the other best-known maker of mechanical bears, Gebrüder Bing, which marketed its products, also from Nuremberg, from the early 1900s.

MERRYTHOUGHT The word 'merrythought' is an antique English term for a wishbone, and that is the trade name and sign of this company, founded in 1930 in the Shropshire town of Ironbridge. Very early Merrythought bears

carry a Steiff-like trade button in the ear, but this soon gave way to a label sewn on to one foot. Merrythought came into being to exploit the use of traditional Yorkshire plush material and was sponsored by a firm of mohair spinners who realized that the new synthetic fibres, such as rayon, represented a threat to their market. Ever since it was founded, Merrythought has enjoyed a reputation for making traditional bears of high quality. A Merrythought exhibition, associated with the Ironbridge Museum, is a source of pleasure to visitors.

INSTANT COLLECTABLES

No leading manufacturer of soft toys is today without its line in teddy bears. There are many bears of fine quality available, both as mass-market products and from workshops specializing in individually hand-crafted toys. From the infant's viewpoint, industrial standards of safety mean that the bear has never been a safer companion. From the collector's viewpoint, there never were so many choices competing for attention.

The essential romanticism of collectors has always led them to take a delight in the way a bear's rought-and-tumble nursery history moulds its battered but unbowed character. It may therefore seem a strange irony that a child's toy can become altogether too valuable an item to be allowed to fall into the hands of children. This, however, is what has happened in the area of designer craft bears or replica bears in limited editions which are made with a specific

RIGHT: *This example of a reproduction bear by Judy Sparrow is traditional even to the hump on the back, as the profile* (BELOW) *shows.*

eye to the collector's market. The traditional collector is likely to view these creations, however handsome they may be, as rather cold fish, and naturally enough, such bears tend to be quite expensive to buy in the first place. Afterwards they need to be maintained in mint condition if they are to remain valuable or possibly rise in value and prove to have been a good investment for their owners.

Steiff were quick to take up the idea of a reproduction vintage bear and in 1980 issued their centenary golden plush bear in a world-wide edition of 11,000 to commemorate their first hundred years of existence as a company. The teddy bear 80th anniversary year of 1983 saw several special issues, one of these being a handsome Steiff bear in silver grey mohair.

Merrythought weighed in with a 'Diamond Jubilee' bear that was a precise replica of the first golden bear they made in 1930. Fitted with a growler, it was limited to 1,000 bears and was exclusive to Harrods.

This section of the collectors' market is certainly an ever-expanding one at the moment, encouraged by the theory that, as soon as an edition of a particular bear has sold out, then the individual bears can be expected to start appreciating in value. Bears are at least a good deal more fun and better for the soul than many other areas of high finance.

Steiff continue to keep their replicas coming on to the market, and of course they have an unrivalled bank of historical and famous bears on which to draw. One of the more interesting of their recent issues is Alfonzo, limited to an edition of 5,000 and exclusive to the shop 'Teddy Bears' of Witney in Oxfordshire, who are the owners of the original. This is an example of a replica which reproduces the 'worn look'. Alfonzo was in May 1989 the proud holder of the world record price for a teddy bear, having been sold at Christie's for £12,100 ($22,000). In fact his record was startlingly eclipsed only four months later by the £55,000 ($100,000) Steiff bear sold at Sotheby's.

In the case of Alfonzo, a small perky bear only 13 inches (32 cm) high and dressed in silk Cossack-style tunic and trousers, his red mohair plush made him a great rarity, but on top of that he benefitted from a romantic provenance. He had belonged to the Princess Xenia Georgievna, a second cousin of the last Tsar of Russia who happened to be staying with the British Royal Family when the Russian Revolution broke out in 1917. Thus Alfonzo escaped the consequences of that historic upheaval and settled down to a life of exile in Britain.

We cannot all become the owners of original vintage Steiffs, and replicas are certainly one way of taking a direct delight in the value and beauty of much of the original workmanship. The bear on the ottoman is more immediate and personal to us than the bear in the museum. Not all limited edition bears are replicas, however. The House of Nisbet, for instance, who worked with the late Peter Bull on various ursine projects, have put out a number of original issues, usually of 5,000 each. They include one of a small Peter Bull bear called 'Bully Minor' and another of Aloysius alias Delicatessen. In the field of replication, Nisbet have also issued a Schuco 'Yes/No' bear. The bears designed by Sue Quinn for her company Dormouse Designs in Scotland may also be cited among limited edition originals of special character, only a few hundred of each design having been manufactured.

Even the experts are hard put to it to explain how the world's currently most expensive bear, a Steiff dating from the 1920s, can have made the sensational price of £55,000 ($100,000) at a Sotheby auction in September 1989. The result seems to have come about through two keen bidders showing an equal determination. Given the present climate of collectors' fever, we therefore constantly need to remind ourselves that what we are dealing with is only a child's toy, not an old master. The collector should certainly keep a serious eye open for those bears that are simply and humbly available in the shops. Nowadays Britain, the United States and Europe all have a thriving craft industry in bears of character. You will soon come to know the names of the firms, workshops or designers whose bears you happen to find personally attractive.

In buying modern bears, as in buying any bear, the question of quality is paramount, both in terms of design and of manufacture. The same rules apply here as in any other area of collecting. You should keep within the limits of what you can afford and the motive of individual appeal should be placed above other considerations. If you buy well then you buy for lasting pleasure, and in 50 or so years' time when your collection of 'vintage' bears is auctioned at Sotheby's, your grandchildren may well thank you for it. Remember, though, to keep safely all documentation relating to a purchase as well as associated tags or labels or other publicity material, for it always adds greatly to the interest and importance of any item to have its provenance fully preserved.

BELOW: *A Dean's Rag Book label* in situ *on the foot of a polar bear teddy.*

9

RESTORING BEARS TO THEIR FORMER GLORY

ASSESSING THE DAMAGE

THE WORDS 'much loved' in an auctioneer's catalogue, when they are used to describe a teddy bear, have come to be a euphemism for 'worn and torn'. Again we need to remind ourselves that the purchaser is buying a child's toy, not a work of art. A certain amount of wear and tear is inevitable in an old bear, though it sometimes happens that you do come across one which has never been played with, perhaps because the child died before it was old enough to enjoy it. Summing up the condition of a bear you are thinking of buying need take only a little practice.

If a bit of restoration work has already been carried out, then this will usually be obvious. When you are buying at auction, however, there is something to be said for buying a bear in an unrestored state so that you can judge, from your own observation, exactly what needs to be

done. A tear in the fabric can be patched, and lost stuffing can be made good. A missing ear or eye can be restored, wool stitching can be put back where it belongs and worn-through pads can be re-covered. None of these tasks is too daunting for the amateur.

It is possible for a bear to be over-restored, either if unsympathetic or unsuitable materials have been used, or if the repair work obscures the original expression or tampers with the proportions of the body or limbs. An attempt to restore an old bear's original colour (which can usually be seen by checking under the arms) would likewise come under the heading of over-restoration. The objective of restoration should never be to cover up or 'correct' those details which give us clues to a bear's life history. If your bear has a head that leans a little to one side or a rather squashed muzzle or a patch of fur worn down with hugging, then that is part of its charm and no true arctophile would wish to correct it. A bear that has been over-restored

ABOVE: *A well-preserved Schuco clockwork tumbling bear from the 1920s.*

133

FACING PAGE: *Two well-loved bears for whom a bit of first-aid and restoration should work wonders.*

LEFT: *A restored bear with unusually luxuriant fur.*

should always be avoided if you find it offered for sale.

Of course, the less that is wrong with a bear, then the more expensive it is going to be to buy. Vintage bears with growlers still in working condition, for instance, are naturally scarcer than those whose growlers have ceased to work. There is always a certain ratio between value and condition in the context of a bear's make or period. So far as the purchaser is concerned the basic adage cannot be over-emphasized: go for what appeals to you, pay no more than you can afford and avoid keeping the notion of 'investment' too much in mind.

BEAR REPAIR

In what circumstances can you undertake your own repair work, and when should you seek the help of experts? If you have been shockingly extravagant and bought yourself an ursine aristocrat costing a small fortune then it goes without saying that you ought to seek expert advice before tampering with it in any way. With less expensive but nevertheless highly desirable bears, on the other hand, there is a good deal of domestic first aid that is practicable for the amateur to consider.

In the life of a bear, patches are as honourable as scars on a soldier. The first important principle, though, is to conserve old materials wherever you can and to match new materials as closely as possible with the old in terms of colouring and texture. If a tear in the fabric needs repairing, then a patch can be neatly stitched over it. If stuffing needs to be replaced, then the same sort of padding should be used, whether it be wood wool, kapok or something else. (Wood wool, incidentally, always seems to make for the sturdiest bears.) Pads often show signs of wear, especially if they are made from

felt. Using a thin matching felt, these should be replaced over the top of the original. If the felt needs to be moulded to fit, then it can first be steamed gently over a kettle.

It quite often happens that one ear has been lost somewhere along the way. In that case, you can carefully unpick the surviving ear to produce two identical and more or less semi-circular halves. These, relined with matching or toning felt, can then form the outer parts for a pair of ears that may be sewn back into position on the head. Treating all conserved and new materials against moths, especially if they are wool or mohair, is a sensible precaution.

Restoring black wool stitching for nose, mouth and claws is one of the simplest tasks. Eyes are

rather more complicated, but matching sets of glass eyes are easy to come by and not difficult to insert or 'spike'. For an older bear, where boot-button eyes may be in character and authentic, you will need to go to some extra trouble to track them down in shops specializing in 'bygones'. Once you have found a supply, they are simple to sew into position.

A particularly serious problem can occur with jointed bears when the cardboard discs that rotate, and so allow a limb to move, rub against and wear through the fabric, so that the limb gets detached. You should inspect any prospective bear carefully to check that this is not happening or about to happen, for here is a problem that even the experts find a challenge.

BELOW: *A bear repair kit includes spare eyes as well as discs for movable heads and limbs and a growler.*

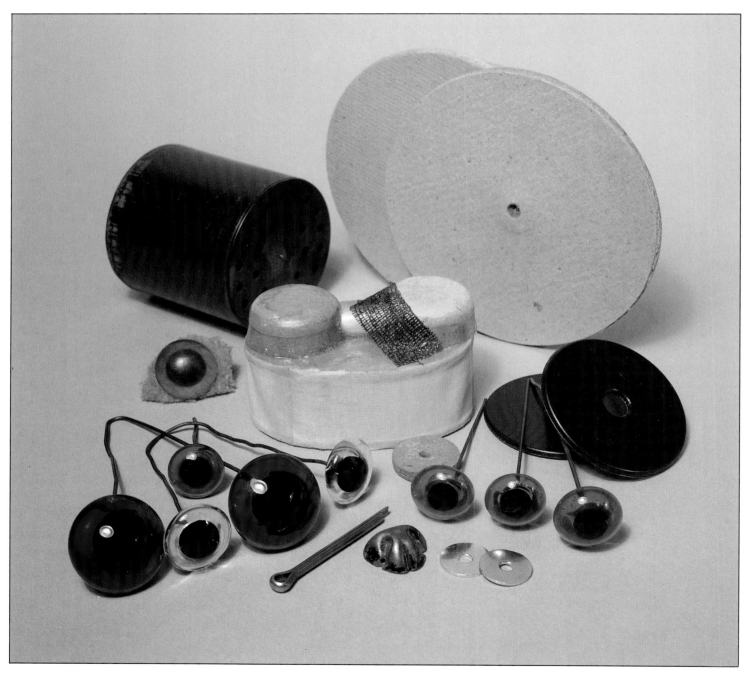

LEFT: *Skating bear, dressed for sport and ready for anything.*

RIGHT: *Can teddy bears grow to resemble their owners?*

If you do take on a bear suffering from this symptom, then you should be aware that it can involve a costly repair; and if a limb does come adrift, then do be careful not to lose it.

BEAR CARE

Teddy bears make wonderful homes for all sorts of pests. Mice, for example, will see a vintage bear, stuffed with excelsior wood wool, as a first-class dwelling. You will need to guard against the disaster which mice could represent, especially if you have to store a bear away for a while for any reason. Bears may also act as host to mites, fleas, silver fish and the dreaded eggs and larvae of the clothes moth. For a newly acquired bear, or even a bear you have had for some time but never treated, it is a good idea to follow Pam Hebbs's advice and place him, sealed in a plastic

bag, for at least two days in a freezer. When you take him out, any condensation can be dried off with a hair dryer on a low setting and his fur carefully brushed. A general moth-proofing is then advisable to ward off further attacks, but any enemies previously present will have been brought to account.

Bears are great dust traps, so they should be gently brushed over every now and then. Keep a special brush to brush out the fur of your bears, for human hair oils do not make good contacts for plush or mohair fibres. The brush should have firm but not harsh or scratchy bristles. It is possible, Pam Hebbs also advises, to shampoo a bear, provided that great care is exercised. The mildest possible fabric shampoo should be sparingly used, slightly diluted and teased lightly into the fur with a nail brush, using circular motions. After towelling the bear with a soft towel, repeat the process with tepid water that contains a recom-

LEFT: *The ultimate accolade for a teddy bear is a child's affection.*

mended proportion of fabric conditioner. Towel the bear once more and then dry with a hair dryer set to give a low heat, brushing delicately as the process continues. Finally the bear can be kept in an airing cupboard for a couple of days before being given a last brisk brushing over.

Damp and light are enemies that the arctophile has in common with the art collector as they may both be as harmful to bears as they can be to pictures. Each hazard is to be avoided. The damage that damp can do is obvious, but light will fade the colour pigments of a fabric (it will probably already have done so on a vintage bear) and direct sunlight may hasten the decay process in natural fibres. Bears are best kept in a shaded position in a room that has a normal level of warmth and humidity.

You will also need to guard your bears against the attentions of other family members, parti-

cularly if there is a cat or a dog who may see them as comfortable cushions. And always put your favourite or valuable bears out of sight before friends with small children visit you. The children will expect to be allowed to play with the bears as soon as they see them, and the parents will expect you to let them do so – quite probably with horrible results. If you often have visits from young families, it may be a good plan to maintain a second-division hug of knockabout bears simply for entertainment purposes.

The last protection to consider is insurance. In every area of collecting, values creep up, and you should double-check with your insurance agent or broker on whether your bear collection needs to be specially listed under your household cover. This seems a wise precaution in times when the value of even one bear can reach considerable heights.

139

· · · · · SELECTED READING LIST · · · · ·

Bull, Peter, **BOOK OF TEDDY BEARS,** Cassell 1977. Expanded version of *Bear With Me* (1969), re-issued as **THE TEDDY BEAR BOOK** (1983).

Cockerell, Pauline, **TEDDY BEARS AS SOFT TOYS,** Shire Publications 1988.

Hebbs, Pam, **COLLECTING TEDDY BEARS,** Collins 1988.

Hillier, Mary. **TEDDY BEARS: A CELEBRATION,** Ebury Press 1985.

Keyes, Josa, **THE TEDDY BEAR STORY,** Windward 1985.

Menton, Ted, **THE TEDDY BEAR LOVERS CATA-LOGUE,** Ebury Press 1984.

Mullins, Linda, **TEDDY BEARS PAST AND PRESENT: A COLLECTOR'S IDENTIFICATION GUIDE,** Hobby Horse Press 1987.

Picot, Geneviève and Gérard, **TEDDY BEARS,** Weidenfeld & Nicolson 1988.

Theobalds, Pam (ed. and illus.) **THE TEDDY BEAR: AN ANTHOLOGY,** Blackie 1988.

Waring, Philippa and Peter, **IN PRAISE OF TEDDY BEARS,** Souvenir Press 1980. Reissued as **TEDDY BEARS** (1985).

INDEX